THE CHILI CONE CHRONICLES

How I Survived the Sixties in Small-Town America

Michael Winslow

iUniverse, Inc.
Bloomington

The Chili Cone Chronicles
How I Survived the Sixties in Small-Town America

iUniverse books may be ordered through booksellers or by contacting:

iUniverse
1663 Liberty Drive
Bloomington, IN 47403
www.iuniverse.com
1-800-Authors (1-800-288-4677)

ISBN: 978-1-4502-7706-8 (pbk)
ISBN: 978-1-4502-7707-5 (cloth)
ISBN: 978-1-4502-7708-2 (ebk)

Printed in the United States of America

iUniverse rev. date: 11/23/2010

Library of Congress Control Number: 2010917729

For my lovely wife LeAna and my three wonderful children,
all of whom came along at the right times in my life…
my cup truly, unequivocally runneth over with love.

This is a non-fiction book. Some names have been changed, some events have been amended and some of the people in it are composites, but by and large this is a book based on true events and real characters.

Truth, after all, is stranger than fiction…

Michael Winslow
September 19, 2010

THANKS, KUDOS & ACKNOWLEDGEMENTS

As with any arduous writing project, the author owes special thanks to a very unique group of individuals. They are, in no particular order:

Dawn, who encouraged me to get the book written when all I could do was conceptualize it.

John Bowes, who actually read chapter after chapter of rough drafts and pushed me along when I faltered.

Rick and Kaye, who took personal interest in assisting me with publishing options—the hardest part of the whole process in my humble opinion.

Mom, for unearthing nuggets of the past that I had simply forgotten or stored away in my mental trunk. Our telephone conversations about people and events 50 years ago brought both smiles and tears—and greatly added to the project.

Tom and Stu and the *Chanute Tribune*.

Older sis for recalling events even Mom and I weren't aware of—and putting up with me that whole decade—especially when I got into her 45 rpm records.

Eric, who never greeted me in the past several years without asking when the book was going to be out.

And to Betti, Carla, Richard, Ben, Robbie, Cindy, Helen and Samson who shared memories of their youth with me, taking me back to a special place at a special time. I hope my book returns the favor.

CONTENTS

"Ah, but I was so much older then
I'm younger than that now"

- From *My Back Pages* by Bob Dylan

WAKING UP WITH SUGARFOOT

IT WAS AS IF HE were kidnapped by the mob or abducted by Martians. Or more likely, forgot to come home from The Knotty Pine, the seedy, rundown tavern by the railroad tracks where he liked to swill Pabst Blue Ribbon with the boys after work. The only thing I knew for sure was that one minute my father was there, and the next minute he was gone—beat up Chevy Apache truck and all. I don't recall, even though I was only four years old at the time, a formal announcement from mom about what had happened.

In any case, in the summer of 1959, after eight years of marital bedlam and domestic turbulence, mom filed for divorce from dad. And from the moment we moved out of the little house with the cupola window at 4th and Lincoln Streets in Erie, Kansas, none of our lives would ever be the same. The first stop for mom and my older and younger sisters and I was an upstairs apartment at 5th and Butler in Erie—just a few blocks from our former home.

Looking out from the kitchen window of our new living quarters, I could still see the old house. I felt if I stared at it long enough, dad would magically come home and move us all back there and everything would return to normal. No matter that, according to my mom, 'normal' was anything but.

I am not sure what the 1,232 other townspeople of Erie thought of mom—a 26 year old divorcee with three kids was not generally thought of in a positive way in that era—but Lloyd Lane, the gaunt, middle aged man who owned the rambling house where our apartment was located—clearly was infatuated with her. We weren't at that address

1

for long, but I remember him acting very peculiar around mom any time he was near her.

Together with acquaintance Chin Moses, they became good friends and spent time visiting, fishing and concocting home brew in Lloyd's claw foot bathtub—the pungent, cider-tinged aroma of which I can still smell to this very day. Little did I know that all the while mom had been carrying on a clandestine romance with an older man in Chanute, Kansas, 16 miles northwest of Erie. Before you could say 'kindergarten' mom was re-married to a stern, humorless man named Bob Wright and we were packing our bags once again—this time for another town.

It was 1960.

Compared to the tiny village of Erie, Chanute was a virtual metropolis of 10,849 residents. I had been regaled with stories of the town teeming with commerce and truck, train and bus traffic—and I couldn't wait to get there to check it all out. Imagine, then, my acute disappointment when learning that the house we would be living at with Bob and his two sons from a previous marriage was actually on the outskirts of town on West Main Street—beyond the city limits.

Problems surfaced, as one might expect in this complex situation, almost immediately. First there was the new family assimilation plan. Or lack of one. Bob's two boys couldn't have been more different from each other. It was as if they were sired by a completely different set of parents.

Butch, the older one, appeared to me at the time to be about 25 years old, though I later learned that he was about 12. He had curly, fiery red hair and a disposition to match. He fought with everyone who came within arm's distance and he had one volume of speech—loud. I had never heard of the idea of demon possession, but in retrospect I believe that something at least very similar was occurring to Butch.

If he was the malevolent Mr. Hyde, then younger brother Jackie was the benevolent Dr. Jekyll. Jackie was everything Butch was not—kind, considerate, polite and caring. He quickly took me under his wing at the little yellow farmhouse on the lonely blacktop. It was to be virtually the only positive thing to come out of the short-lived relationship between our two families. He introduced me to comic books, taught me how to ride a bike, bait a fishing line and most important of all—how to avoid being maimed or killed by Sugarfoot.

Sugarfoot was an ugly, mangy, smelly nanny goat that the Wright's kept on their property for some heretofore unknown reason. There was precious little grass to eat, nor was there an abundance of noxious weeds or woody shrubs and trees. She didn't appear to be providing milk, and because she was still very much alive, there was no meat to be gleaned from her, either. I soon learned that she was the 'guard' goat and her only responsibility in life was to clear the property of intruders or wayfarers.

Unfortunately, because she was a goat with a brain the size of a pebble of sand, Sugarfoot wasn't able to properly differentiate between interlopers and inhabitants. Thus, we were all fair game for her attacks, which were swift, precise and final. I don't remember the exact circumstance, but I can recall the first time she laid me out. Seeing her, I froze out in the middle of the yard, paralyzed by fear, and watched as she rumbled toward me with her head down, her horizontal, slit-shaped pupils fixated on my skinny five-year-old body. It was as if I were hit by a diesel locomotive at 60 miles per hour.

The force of the impact knocked me clear out of my shoes, and I laid there doing my best to play dead, hoping she would go away. Strange thing was—she did go away. Apparently, and this was to be useful information for future run-ins with her, once she had taken you down, the thrill was gone. She was content to move on—probably in search of other, new victims in her insatiable wanderlust for blood.

That first encounter was merely that—a *first* encounter. No matter how stealthily I moved about the property or how carefully I planned my route to my bicycle, mailbox or the street out front, Sugarfoot always seemed to materialize out of nowhere, barreling at me like Green Bay Packer tackle Forrest Gregg, intent on separating me from my senses. Sometimes I played the role of the crooked prizefighter taking a dive and making good on a fix, voluntarily hitting the ground just to deprive her of the moment. It was great fun to watch her as she tried to figure out what just happened—and more importantly—what to do next. Usually she just sauntered off with a look of bewilderment on her bearded face, occasionally looking back as if she had left something important behind.

It was a shame, really. The rest of the world was concerning itself with grave events of the day. Francis Gary Powers had been captured by the Russians when they shot down his Lockheed U-2 Dragon Lady spy plane. Sputnik 4 was launched into the earth's orbit. A terrible

3

earthquake, still one of the greatest to ever occur, tore Chile apart from Talcahuano to the Taitao Peninsula. I, on the other hand, on my little island and totally oblivious to critical world events, was waging a battle of wits with a four-legged machine of destruction.

As time went by, though, I gradually figured her out and began to outthink the old goat. On the increasingly rare occasions where she successfully ran me down or cornered me on the porch (one of her favorite moves) mom would come to the rescue, firing hedge apples at her, boinking her on the head and distracting her long enough so that I could escape. I could never understand why Sugarfoot didn't just eat all of the hedge apples, thereby depriving my mother of the ammunition cache that would eventually be used against her. Goats, I knew, had amazing digestive systems.

In any case, the encounters between the old goat and myself ebbed over time. I began to cautiously, delicately enjoy the daily bike rides to Lincoln Elementary School, a half-mile into town, and occasional forays with Jackie downtown to Zip Drug, where we would chug Root Beer floats and read comics from the racks in air-conditioned comfort until management prodded us to "buy or be gone."

The atmosphere in the little house on West Main Street gradually grew more tense, though, and always seemed on the verge of implosion. I could never figure out why—it was just starting to get fun for me. In retrospect, I suppose it was difficult for everybody involved—seven people suddenly cloistered together in very tight quarters, strangers to one another.

Mom had, at best, a rocky relationship with Bob. Margaret, my older sister, appeared sad and perpetually unhappy. Deirdre, my younger sister, laid low and did her best not to be seen or heard. Butch fought with everybody. Sugarfoot continued to stalk—even with varied results. I found sanctuary only with Jackie. He was the big brother I never had, the person that I needed the most—even if he was just a step-brother. And all that was about to change.

One windblown and overcast February morning in 1961, teachers at Lincoln collectively noticed with some dismay that none of us five kids were in attendance at school that day. Rightfully assuming that something might be very wrong, the authorities were dispatched to our house. Noting that the family vehicle was in the driveway but no one was answering the door, and I suppose, fearing foul play, a decision was made to break into the house.

It was a good call to say the least. All of us were found unconscious in our beds. Some of us had vomited in our sleep. It took quite a bit of time before they were able to rouse Bob and mom from their sepulchral slumber.

One by one, the rest of us were all woken up and transported to Neosho Memorial Hospital for examination. The initial test results indicated carbon monoxide poisoning. A faulty furnace heat exchanger had emitted dangerous levels of the odorless, tasteless and toxic gas throughout the house via the ductwork system. It would be several days before any of us children felt normal enough to return to classes nor the adults to work. Hadn't it been for the keen response of vigilant school and law enforcement officials, you might not be reading this book. For me, however, it was but one of two near-death experiences while living with the Wrights. And Sugarfoot, I am happy to report, had nothing to do with either.

The following June we made a rare trip to Santa Fe Lake, south of town, to picnic, fish and swim. These outings were cherished and helped, at least for me, to take the sting out of not seeing dad anymore. Soon after setting up camp, Butch, Jackie and I headed over to the boat dock and ramp to drop our lines and try our luck there. We were having a great time fishing, talking and joking—even Butch seemed unusually happy that day. The gentle lapping of the water up against the pier was a lyrical soundtrack.

There were some support beams jutting off the side of the dock that had once been covered by lake water—but were now visible due to a paucity of spring rains. Craving a better casting vantage point, I decided to take a walk out on one of the beams. The water in that cove was not very deep—perhaps 8-10', but it may as well have been 80' deep to a six year old who didn't know how to swim.

When I lost my footing and slipped from the beam into the water, the first thing I did was let go of my fishing pole and open my eyes—and then try to breathe. I remember how *green* the water looked—and how different it appeared from *below* the surface. Then, as I began sucking water into my lungs instead of air, I panicked. I flailed away in the emerald foam assured that I was going to die. After what seemed like an eternity, but was in fact just a few seconds, someone crashed into the water beside me, cradled me in their arms and towed me safely to the shore.

Butch—not Jackie—had saved my life. I would never again think of him as the recalcitrant, mean-tempered step-brother always spoiling for a fight. He was, at least on that sunny, early summer day at the lake, my guardian angel. And for the second time in six months, I had cheated death—unless, of course, you happen to count all of the near-misses with Sugarfoot.

The final dissolution and break-up of mom's marriage to Bob was eerily familiar to that of hers with my dad. We got no warning, no speech and no preparation. One day we were there in the little yellow house on West Main Street and the next we were moving into an upstairs apartment on South Evergreen Street. It was no wonder that I eventually began to equate apartments with separation.

Déjà vu, divorce-style.

Just when I had gotten somewhat contented with my new family and the only school that I had ever known, we were on our own again—mom, sisters and I. It would be a very long time before I got over not seeing Jackie everyday. He did ride his bicycle over to our apartment a few times, which amazed me, as it was at least five miles from the old house.

I even missed old cranky, argumentative Butch, always reminding myself of the day he saved my life. But there would be a new school to attend, Roosevelt Elementary, money would get increasingly tight for mom and we would all have to make new friends. We had no car and no telephone. We were literally strangers in a strange land.

At least there were no goats in the yard.

SIGHTS, SOUNDS, SMELLS &
STRANGE CHARACTERS

AT ABOUT THE SAME TIME we moved into the city of Chanute proper—and perhaps it was an inexplicable coincidence with my attending first grade at Roosevelt—I began to be acutely aware of all of the sensory wonders of our new environs. From the shrieking shift change whistle at Mid-America Refinery on the north end of town to the idyllic church bells of the stately First Presbyterian Church on Main Street, the town seemed to be governed, and indeed moved along by sounds.

Unlike sleepy little Erie, downtown Chanute was bristling with hurried pedestrians, honking cars and hungry parking meters. Semi tractor trailer trucks growled through town on U.S. 169, grinding gears and spewing plumes of acrid smoke as they snaked north and south, crossing Main Street at the dead center. Up and down the narrow concrete corridor, from such filling stations as Deep Rock, DX and Sinclair, the pleasant noise of impact wrenches spinning off lug nuts in the garages and the "ding-ding" of their driveway air hoses were an antithesis to the traffic drone.

Diesel horns blasted from the Santa Fe Railroad switching yards just a couple of blocks west of the heart of town. Nothing could compare, though, to the ear-splitting sounds of box cars slamming into one another in the hump yard. It was not, I imagined, unlike those of a hydrogen bomb. The yard, I soon learned, was a virtual city within a city of unusual sounds—hissing air brakes, squealing wheel bearings, rails that moaned, humming refrigerator cars and the constant and ever-present grinding of the engines as they plied their service. It was all a wonderful discordance—a tapestry of blue collar music, if you will—that would have an immediate and lasting impact upon me.

In and around June of each year, the soft whishing sound of wheat and grains being loaded into rail cars from the elevators at Chanute Grain & Seed were an auditory reminder that summer had commenced. It was a real treat to see, like clockwork, the procession of trucks laden with grain being weighed, unloading their bounty and then seeing the product finally being hauled off in oxidized rail cars to parts unknown by trademark yellow and blue ATSF engines.

Everywhere I looked—and I looked everywhere those first few years in Chanute—the sounds of a city very much alive greeted me. Forklifts churned in the lumber yards, school bells kept the youthful masses in line, airplanes took off and landed at the small airport west of town, and every once in a while wailing sirens from Police or Fire Department vehicles would pierce the air.

Until that time, I had never known a city could *smell*, too. I didn't recall any particular odors from the time I had lived in Erie—but this was something very different. For starters, the refinery spewed a variety of foul-smelling vapors, and if the wind happened to be blowing from the north, its fumes would permeate the entire north end of town. Not surprisingly, some of Chanute's poorest families lived nearest the refining complex where the odors became part of everyday life—olfactory white noise.

If the aromas from Mid-America Refinery were the most significant in town, those that emanated from the concrete-walled drainage ditch that ran along Second Street from the west side of the city to the east were surely second. It was referred to as "the Sewer," though it was in reality a canal full of rocks, water, trash and broken glass. It had a dank, musty and distinctly 'sewer-like' smell about it which no young boy in town could resist. It beckoned to us with its siren call of stench like some primeval Svengali.

Periodic rainstorms sometimes altered the milieu of the ditch, rearranging its topography and shifting the fetid pools of water. Thus, it became a virtual new experience nearly every time following a thunderstorm. One of my most cherished memories as a youth was to see, shortly after a torrential rain had dumped nine inches of rain on the city in a twelve-hour span, a perfectly good sofa, cushions intact, careening eastward in the ditch, which had become a dangerous, churning river the color of chocolate milk. It passed under the bridge on South Forest Street like an out-of-control, navigator-less kayak and was gone before you could say "houndstooth."

There were seasonal smells that synchronized the city more tightly and in a way no fine timepiece ever could. In the spring, the air was a perfume of freshly-mowed grass, lavender, blooming and flowering shrubs and trees. Chlorine and Coppertone wafting from the Municipal Swimming Pool were harbingers of summer. The broiling July sun drew the creosote out of the railroad ties down at the Santa Fe yards. In the fall, it was the pungent smell of burning leaves and of furnaces being fired up after a few months rest. Winter brought wood smoke bitter on the wind and the smell of cedars bracing against the cold.

The most compelling facet of this new place to me, though, was visual. It looked nothing like Erie—the only town I had ever lived in. In fact, the only other place I had ever been was to Salem, Indiana to visit paternal Grandparents, in 1958. And Salem was *smaller* than Erie. Compared to them, Chanute was a metropolis.

It even had its own skyscraper—The Tioga Hotel—a six-story art deco building constructed in 1929 that sat at Main and Lincoln in the heart of downtown. From each corner of the very top of the hotel, four sinister-looking concrete grotesques peered down on the city. It was, of course, every boy's dream—aside from successfully traversing the Sewer—to get to the roof of the tallest building in Chanute and look down with the grotesques.

There were three ways up to the roof.

One was via the elevator to the 6th floor. That meant getting by Jenkins, the uniformed, black elevator attendant. "Which floor?" he would ask the rider initially. Then, more pressing, he would lean down with narrowed, ebony eyes and whisper, "Who are you here to see, Sir?" As most eight year olds didn't have an answer for the latter, he would then casually escort them off of the elevator—even before it had departed for upper floors—and out onto the sidewalk.

The stairs were also an option, but as their entrance was but a few feet from the elevator and the all-seeing Jenkins, most of us kids eschewed this preference. Besides, even if he wasn't around, there was usually some snoopy busy-body standing guard behind the registration desk, keen to the machinations of grade school boys.

The third, and by far the most dangerous, option was the fire escape ladder which zigzagged up the north side of the hotel with its breathtaking view of the alley and dumpsters below. Which is precisely where I always pictured myself falling to after contemplating the rusted railings and grating. There was no Jenkins or registration desk pit bull to stop anyone who dared to try. Many were the cumulative hours that I stood in the passage, staring at the fading paint on the bars and rungs—trying to summon enough courage to make the climb. Even the grotesques seemed to taunt me. As it turned out, I never did get to the roof.

Aside from the Tioga, the rest of the downtown area, while clean and pretty, was very aseptic, and presented few challenges for curious boys. There were clothing stores, shoe stores, a Kress store, a Ben Franklin, a corner drug store (Zip Drug) and a cool hardware store that still had the original wooden floor and pressed tin ceilings. The two barbershops on Main also doubled as shoe-shine parlors, and one of them had a great gimmick for kids—they *traded* comic books. If you brought one in, you could take one out at no charge. It was, of course, the barbershop of choice for the majority of Chanute's grade schoolers.

There was an ice plant on East First Street that always fascinated us, too. It looked like a great place to work in the summer. I was always curious what their employees did all winter, though, when ice was both abundant and *free*. Across the street there was a hatchery. Yes, a hatchery. Further down the street, there was a curious little shop with a dirt floor where the old proprietor bought all types of metal and wire. He also paid bounties for coyote ears. I have since wondered what kind of background he had come from to mix such unrelated trades.

At the City's sprawling red brick Power Plant complex, it was a fascinating sight to see the huge wooden cooling towers belching heat from their centrifugal fans—especially in the winter when the rejected vapors would freeze on nearby telephone wires and trees. Every once in a while I would summon up enough courage to step up to one of the ground floor windows and peer in to see the physical plant with its humming compressors and huge turbines. The buzz of machinery soon became the theme of this young boy's life.

Looking back, aside from all the sensory wonders, it was virtually inconceivable that any other place had such an abundance of strange and oddball characters per capita than my hometown. My first experience with one of these creatures was when I was taken to F & M Diner by mom's new boyfriend. F & M was much like the diners of old—cramped, smoky, noisy and absolutely glorious—with one row of barstools and plenty of patrons in waiting. Lou, the cook in traditional white smock and stovepipe chef's cap, was a gadfly with an ominous black eye patch. Of course I thought it was a gimmick, so I asked him one morning over a short stack plate why he wore a patch. He never responded—merely leaned forward slowly and lifted the eye patch to reveal a gleaming, pure white eye. No iris, no cornea, no pupil. Just a filmy, white eyeball. I had nightmares for about a month after that and still can't eat pancakes to this day.

Then there was Red the Hobo who purportedly came to town on a Katy freight train one stormy night and decided to stay a while. We weren't sure where he lived—it was rumored that he had a campfire in an old abandoned city building near Katy Park on the east side of town. He was stooped, poorly dressed and had a sing-song demeanor which totally contradicted his lot in life. It was his full-time occupation to avoid work or any other useful activity. To which, I must say, he was highly successful.

Patty had once been Patrick – Patrick Jackson, that is. Prominent Adam's Apple or not, she paraded down the city streets and shopped unashamedly in the city stores adorned in the most garish women's dresses, hats and shoes—oblivious to the stares and whispers and catcalls. Everyone, including this writer as a seven year old boy, *knew* Patty was actually a man. What impressed me most about Patty was the courage with which he/she displayed just by being in public in a small town during that time period. That took *cojones*—no pun intended.

Jon Triggs was a male of indeterminate age who rode a maroon 1950's style bicycle complete with basket, light and horn. That alone would have been enough to have oneself deemed a quirky character in Chanute, Kansas in 1962. Unfortunately, he looked like the Phantom of the Opera who had suddenly decided to take up farming. His face, due I was sure to some unknown unfortunate medical malady, was sadly deformed—and he wore cuffed blue jeans and a denim jacket with a hunter's cap. He could often be found on any of the various downtown street corners straddling his J.C. Higgins bike with a transistor radio held firmly to his ear. And when he wasn't busy trying to peek under the mannequin's dresses in the J.C. Penney storefront window, he was entertaining crowds of young people with his ability to blow his nose unabashedly into his bare hands without the need for a kerchief.

In those days, we had only one movie theater in town—The People's Theater on East Main Street. It was built in 1928 by the Boller Brothers, had a seating capacity of about 900 and by the time of my youth was beginning its slow slide into disrepair and eventual oblivion. Like Captain Smith of the *HMS Titanic*, Ray Welch was the very visible, able and capable manager of an ultimately doomed enterprise. He was slight, bald, bespectacled and, to us adversarial kids, had the appearance and personality of a kindly but curmudgeon uncle.

His chief claim to fame was how often he thwarted unruly patrons such as my friends and I from gaining access to the balcony section of the theater. Wizened beyond his years, he took great pride in blazing his sleek, black 100 Watt flashlight into our eyes, causing an immediate and long-lasting blinding effect. He knew it was much easier to herd a group of troublemaking boys back down the stairs to the lobby with their sight gone, perhaps forever.

During these highly charged emotional confrontations the great captain would invariably lecture us on the dangers of raining Jujubee's and Slow Poke sticks down onto the ground floor audience. Occasionally we were asked to sit with him on the stairs and think about our actions and how they affected others. It had, I am now ashamed to admit, no real lasting impression on us. The war of sticky candy, unwary theater-goers and cat-and-mouse with Ray would rage on unabated for years.

On a positive note, my sight has started to return—slowly.

Orley's Café arguably had the best chili and pinball machines in town. The place was owned and operated by Orley and his wife Delores. Orley himself was pretty tame—an aging guy who we assumed was from the old country, Italia. He tended to the grill with a big metal spatula and a cigarette that was ¾ ash dangling from his lip. He made sure that every table had a decanter of vinegar on it for his signature chili. Delores, on the other hand, glowered with a Methuselah-like intensity and took cadaverous charm and delight in expelling kids from the premises if they so much as laughed or even smiled. Things got so bad for my buddies and I that we had to eventually disguise ourselves with fake noses and horn-rimmed glasses to get in to play pinball.

One of our favorite places to re-enact World War II battles was

Elmwood Cemetery, the city's largest burial grounds. As we lived nearby and the cemetery was a vast expanse of indigenous trees, hills, fencerows, old gravestones and buildings, it was nearly ideal for our skirmishes—except when one of the many groundskeepers flushed us out. Claude was the lone crewman who not only would not expel us from the property—he would even regale us with his own personal World War II experiences.

As time went by, Claude got demonstrably friendlier and actually began to seek us out. He took us down by the duck pond and demonstrated his mastery of a classic wrestling move, the sleeper hold, on a few of the braver kids. He paid our way and accompanied us to swim at the city pool and offered to take us all "camping in the wilderness" with him. It didn't take very long for Claude's unusual interest in a gaggle of young boys to reach one of the mothers. Not surprisingly, we soon learned that Claude wasn't Claude at all, had never fought in the war and was wanted by the authorities on a number of charges relating to contributing to the delinquency of minors. He disappeared after the news broke, and at least for my platoon, it was back to the trenches—and to escaping the clutches of the other groundskeepers.

Perhaps the oddest character of them all, though, wasn't even human. He was Simian.

In the heart of the depression, the Works Progress Administration, a national relief program that provided jobs and income to the unemployed, built quite a few buildings and constructed a number of roads in Chanute. One of their most striking creations was Monkey Island, a flagstone castle, complete with lily-pad moat in the heart of Katy Park. Later, an aviary was added nearby and the little town without a zoo suddenly seemed very cosmopolitan.

Over the years, though, the staggering challenge of maintaining the structure and its inhabitants—and their inherent cost—began to chip away at the city's budget. By the early 1960s Monkey Island was in full free-fall. The moat was murky and the rock turret of the castle was crumbling. Even the monkeys looked depressed and took to smoking cigarettes and throwing feces at visitors. The city fathers finally strangled the unique tourist attraction to death by 1970 and all of the animals—now including goats—were removed and relocated.

Shortly thereafter, Monkey Island was razed. Eventually, a parking lot was built on the spot.

One of the monkeys, Homer, ended up being adopted by a kindly farm family who lived east of Chanute. While it is unknown if Homer was put to work baling hay or picking green beans, it was rumored that he had a special penchant for riding the pigs and goats cowboy-style and could be seen playing on the tire swing in the back yard. He was even issued a driver's license in the name of "Mr. M" from the Kansas Highway Patrol.

From Monkey Island to Green Acres, he gave us all a lesson in patient survival, I suppose.

Whether it was lying in bed on a cold, starless November night listening to the reassuring honks of the Canadian Geese churning south in v-formation seemingly right over our roof or the sight of Train 48, The Oil Flyer, picking up speed as it raced over the Third Street overpass, being in the new city those first few years transmitted an abundance of impulses to my young brain that would burn forever deep in my psyche.

And this was all before I had my first chili cone.

THE LEGEND OF THE CHILI CONE

IT WAS NOT ON A par with, say, the discovery of the laws of refraction or the role of oxygen in respiration and photosynthesis, but make no mistake about it, finding and eating my first chili cone marked a turning point in my young life. It is not diminished by the fact that I cannot remember how I found it or who I was with when I enjoyed my first one.

The chili cone was just that—an Eat-It-All ice cream cone filled with hot chili. It was but one of a flavorful menu of culinary oddities offered at Barker's Dairy Bar, a little mom-and-pop eatery just off Main Street at the corner of South Santa Fe and First Streets. Barker's itself was a wondrous curiosity. For one, it sat at an oddball, peculiar angle on the squared block—completely out of synch with all of the other buildings. And it couldn't make up its mind if it wanted to be an eat-in establishment or take-out. So it became both.

Outside the order window was a short row of dilapidated, weather-worn Naugahyde chairs the color of deep blue metallic that hardly anyone ever sat on. The upholstery was peeling off in places and the seats were constantly damp from rain. Inside were several wrought iron tables that were once painted black—before the names of thousands of teenagers were scrawled on them to the point where there was literally no finish left. I later learned it was a virtual right of passage, and almost a requirement, to carve one's name on the tables. The owners cheerfully looked the other way in tacit approval.

There was a requisite Rock-ola jukebox in the back room along with several wooden high-back booths—of which you were NOT to scratch your name on—and a pinball machine that, over the years, nearly bankrupted me without ever giving me a free replay. Despite the cozy and slightly ethereal ambiance of the place, the best thing of all, though, about Barker's was and forever would be the chili cone and a basket of Susie-Q's.

According to legend, the chili cone concept began in Texas and had been around for many years as a staple of drive-in movie theater concessionaires. I knew of no other place in Chanute that sold the unique food item—not even at our own outdoor cinema, Neo-Cha Drive-in. I never could figure out how they could ladle hot chili into a cone and have it stay crisp while being eaten. It has to be one of science's greatest mysteries—right up there with how the construction of the Pyramids at Giza was executed without machinery.

So pervasive was this unusual treat that the only other gastronomic curiosities to rival the chili cone were the spudnut, which could be found at The Silver Grill, an upscale eatery on Main Street, and the twelve-for-a-dollar Bar-B-Q Sandwich, sold only on Saturdays at Self Service Grocery.

The spudnut, brought to mainland United States in 1940 by brothers Al and Bob Pelton of Salt Lake City, was a doughnut made from potato flour. It was still wildly popular in the 1960s and franchisees sprung up like weeds in a vacant lot. The Silver Grill, where finer dress was expected, was a licensee—and made and sold the confection by the metric ton to yearning customers. I especially liked the sack that the doughnuts came in—with the creepy Mr. Spudnut, looking very much like Mr. Potato Head, on the front tipping his top hat with one hand while gripping his cane with the other.

I have never seen a potato that looked good in a bow tie.

Nearly every Saturday of my youth mom would drag me downtown to enact the role of pack mule to haul groceries back home. Actually, as we did not have a car, it was an easy choice—help or don't eat. Normally I considered it indentured servitude, but every once in a while we would go to a little meat market on the corner of Main Street and Evergreen called Self Service Grocery. Their slogan was "right on the price, right on the corner, right on your way home."

Well, it might have been on someone else's way home, but ours was 14 blocks away and it always involved carting heavy sacks across brick streets and over broken sidewalks. What made this little grocery store atypical was a broiling white cauldron of Bar-B-Q beef that they set up and dispensed to the general public every Saturday—at the unheard of rate of twelve sandwiches for a dollar. Of this I am sure—a better barbecue beef sandwich has never been created. I don't know how they did it, or what ingredients went into the simmering, brown vat, but the result was the best, and cheapest, barbecue beef sandwich in history.

This was a perfect lunch for a mother of three on a budget. And it made the tedious, weary trip to the grocery store much more enjoyable, that's for sure.

These were the days before the invasion of the chain restaurants—and subsequent demise of the mom-and-pop eateries—and there were plenty of other wonderful places to eat, with menus chock full of delicious food. Orley's Café, mentioned earlier, offered great 15-cent hamburgers, Delores's delicious homemade lemon meringue pie and, of course, the most fantastic chili—albeit sans the cone.

Erma's Café, the only restaurant owned and operated by a black family in the city, featured slow-cooked, smoked ribs, steaks and hamburgers. It was always a treat to travel east on Main Street near the Katy Park entrance and pass through a cloud of smoke that was soaked in the aroma of lean meats. That was as close as I ever got as a youngster to actually eating anything from Erma's, though. Mom's budget had no allowances for ribeye or New York strip. We could hardly afford bologna.

The Busy Bee Café, long a staple of downtown Chanute, was situated right by the Santa Fe Railroad tracks and was famous for its lunch counter intimacy, breakfasts and sandwiches. Hart's Café, right down Main Street to the east, had the very best open-face roast beef sandwiches, complete with a mountain of mashed potatoes and brown gravy that I had ever eaten.

La Rosa De Oro was the only Mexican restaurant in the city at the time and the food was so good that it attracted people from all over southeast Kansas. My older sister would move away from Chanute in 1969 to marry and relocate to western Kansas, but every time she came back home for a visit, she did not leave until she had purchased several containers of La Rosa's one-of-a-kind queso dip. To eat there as a kid was a special treat—they even had a fountain in the lobby with lights that changed colors.

The Orchid Buffet was located out west on Cherry Street and

featured family-style home cooking. This establishment was a favorite of the church crowd and was always bustling on Sunday afternoons. I don't recall ever having eaten there as a child just because it was so far out west—and we didn't have a car to get there. I just remember hearing folks talk about how great the food was. And I loved the name of the place—it conjured up images of flower-bedecked buffets and throngs of people dressed in their Sunday finest.

The Sunflower Café was another restaurant on the outposts of the city—northeast of Mid-America Refinery at the very edge of town. It seemed like it never closed because trucks snaking down U.S. 169 stopped there at all hours of the night and day. I remember coming home from the drive-in very late one night and seeing, through bleary eyes, a full parking lot and lights blazing from every window much like an Edward Hopper painting.

Other fine places to eat were the Royal Burger Bar, the King Drive-in with their Big Boy Hamburgers and Pizza Burgers, Bill's Carry-Out (listed in the Polk directory at the time of being in the *rear* of 924 North Santa Fe,) Big Burger Bar, Drumstick Café, Home Lunch and White Grill Restaurant.

Of course it was very rare that we ever got to eat out, but every once in a while one of mom's beaus would treat us all to a trip to one of these wonderful greasy spoons. It certainly beat the usual supper fare at our house, which most often consisted of boiled cabbage, navy beans and cottage cheese. Mom could fix these three entrees in about 50 different ways—even to the point where you didn't realize what you were eating was in fact cabbage, navy beans and cottage cheese. It was a gift, I swear.

There weren't many places to eat near our little apartment on Evergreen Street, but I savored any and every chance to test them all when the opportunity presented itself.

None of the eateries or their offerings ever really challenged for my heart (or stomach) like Barker's Dairy Bar and the chili cone, though. Whether it was a sultry summer afternoon or a gloomy, overcast winter evening, nothing ever hit the spot quite like it.

I wonder if anyone has yet contemplated a chili *waffle* cone.

IN THE NEIGHBORHOOD

As HAD BEEN THE PATTERN for the first six years of my life, we didn't stay too long at the apartment on South Evergreen with the sprawling Catalpa tree and its beans and fragrant, yellow-white blooms, out front. Still, in such a short time, my mom would accomplish much—and it felt like we were joining the human race at last. Translation—we got our first television set. It was 1962.

Used, little and problem-laden as it was, I was nevertheless overjoyed to see it arrive that sultry spring day. It was not often that I was allowed to watch it—being third on the seniority chart—but early on I began cultivating an interest in local and world news. As you can imagine, this was somewhat disconcerting to my mother, who much preferred that I watch *The Three Stooges* or *Our Gang* reruns or *Leave It To Beaver*.

I was, unfortunately, enthralled with *The Huntley-Brinkley Report*, NBC television network's flagship evening news program. Instead of gravitating toward kid show staples like *Captain Kangaroo* and *Popeye*, I instead found some unexplained comfort in the dour delivery of Chet Huntley and David Brinkley—and the way they said "goodnight" to each other at the close of the program.

I practiced saying "goodnight" like them to my little sister every night.

"Your friends are not going to want to talk about Telstar or the fallout from the Bay of Pigs invasion," my mother warned me, as if I had friends to bore. Sure, I had some schoolmates that I hung out with once in awhile, and there was a smattering of neighborhood ne'r-do-wells, but we never talked about world events. Mostly, our conversations centered around how to come up with enough coinage to go to Warner's Grocery and buy candy. For the most part, I kept the Cold War, riots and plane crashes to myself.

We had all of three channels to choose from in those days, an NBC affiliate and one for CBS and ABC respectfully. My favorite local programming came from KOAM-TV 7 Pittsburg, the NBC station. They had a children's show that came on every weekday morning called "The Fun Club" that was hosted by Roger Neer, one of the station's newscasters. The unquestionable star, though, was a former Hollywood western film extra Lloyd "Slim" Andrews, also known affectionately as 'the 49er.'

"The Fun Club" was his to ride off into the sunset with—and he did so with unabashed relish, performing in full cowboy regalia as a one-man band, puppeteer and eventually host. No one played the kazoo with more conviction and earnest than the 49er. And no one was better at communicating with an assembly of squirming, nervous kids on a television set.

I watched "The Fun Club" nearly every morning as I was getting dressed to go to school that spring, always wondering how the kids on the show got to skip out of their schools. Naturally, I grew to despise those kids.

I loved, however—and not surprisingly—their evening local news show. Vic Cox handled the sports and looked like he might have once played middle linebacker in college. Now nearly bald and wearing a sport jacket, he delivered the sports news and outdoor journals with a matter-of-fact tonality that made me want to take up tennis and try fly-fishing.

The weather was anchored by Earl Ludlum, an immensely popular man who taught math at the local university. He looked every bit the college professor, too, with his ill-fitting suits, bottle-thick glasses and calm, deliberate demeanor. These were the days before computer-generated graphics and orbital satellite technologies, but Earl magically brought to life high pressure centers, cold fronts and temperatures on a Plexiglas cover with a simple grease pencil. And it was through him that I saw my first weather radar—which looked very much like a sonar device that I imagined I was viewing while in my submarine prowling the Baltic Sea for Russian trawlers smuggling arms caches.

One thing is for sure—Earl Ludlum set a standard that all future meteorologists would follow.

By far, though, the most unusual and entertaining show was "Melody Matinee," a low-budget, live country music program hosted by the venerable Lou Martin that came on at lunchtime every weekday. It featured Virgil on the guitar, Bill on the ukulele (yes, ukulele) and the redoubtable Connie Conrad on the Hammond organ playing a menagerie of ancient folk songs that only my grandparents could appreciate and sing along with. For the rest of us, it was sheer torture— and one of the chief reasons I never stayed home from school when I was ill.

Mom made sure that I didn't overdose on TV by sending me outside to play everyday—disregarding tornado warnings, blizzards and plagues of locusts. As Warner's Grocery was just three houses down and at the corner of 14th and Evergreen, it became a key hangout for me, my sisters and the few vagabonds that I called friends. Warner's was the quintessential mom-and-pop corner grocery store—and much more.

For starters, the front screen door that made a 'whack!' on the way in and out of the store had the blue rabbit mascot from Bunny Bread plastered across it. While my sisters thought he was "cute," I found his visage a little more disturbing. He had buck teeth, wore white gloves and was winking as if to say, "Do you need a little spending money?" I could almost see little mites crawling around in his floppy blue and yellow ears.

Inside, there was as much groceries and mercantile as the Warner family could cram into the old ramshackle building as possible. Naturally, the isles were narrow and cramped. They even had their own meat department, complete with glass display cases and sawdust floor. A full array of foodstuffs could be purchased there, including breakfast cereals, soups, cake mixes, spices, sugar, baking soda, etc. Local farmers would also bring in seasonal fresh fruits and vegetables, as well.

It was every kid's dream, too, as we could get all of the icons of childhood there—construction paper, candy, soda pop, small toys, comic books and ice cream bars among others. To peruse their candy racks was to peer into Nirvana itsself. There were Fizzies, Boston Baked Beans, Bazooka Bubble Gum, Kits, Bit-O-Honey's, Bubblegum Cigars, Red Hots, Chick-O-Sticks, Slow Pokes, Necco Wafers, Sugar Babies and many more.

In the soda pop section, other than the ubiquitous Coke and Pepsi products, there were Double Cola, Bubble Up, Dr. Pepper, Shasta, Nehi, Kickapoo Joy Juice, Sun Crest, Simba and Vess among others. Chanute even had its own little bottling company owned by the Legge family, and when they weren't cranking out Dr. Pepper products, their brand, called Legge Beverage, could also make its way onto the shelves of the local grocery stores in a variety of fruity flavors.

The Warners were kind and gracious proprietors who lived just down the block from their store. It was truly a family affair and they knew every neighborhood kid and their parents by name. They even decorated the storefront windows (the store's *only* windows) for the holidays—whether it be soap drawings of ghastly witches for Halloween or a cotton ball snow scene at Christmas. This was a time, it is important to remember, before the large chain grocery stores snaked their way into the small towns across America and forever changed the way we purchased our necessities.

Though it was the twilight of the corner grocery store, Chanute in 1962 was still teeming with them. Warner's just happened to be the one nearest our little apartment on South Evergreen.

The end of the school year marked the beginning of a languid summer filled with boring days and even more boring nights. In June, I stepped on a broken pop bottle submerged under a torrent of rainwater rushing down the curbside in front of our house. The shards created a laceration so severe that I nearly lost the second toe on my right foot and had to wear a cast for several weeks. Therefore, I could not swim nor do anything fun for about a month.

I soon learned that the worst thing about being injured and having to stay indoors was daytime television. As a diversion to such daytime classics as "Melody Matinee" and the various quasi-intellectual soap operas, I discovered, via my older sister's transistor radio, AM-71 WHB radio and popular music. WHB, which stood for "world's happiest broadcasters," was one of the country's pioneering Top 40 format stations and was headquartered in the old Power & Light building in downtown Kansas City, 100 miles north of Chanute. It wasn't long before I was emulating Bobby Vinton and Chubby Checker and singing the station's jingles.

I lost count of the nights that I went to sleep that summer with the little transistor radio next to my ear on the pillow, to the sweet, gentle sounds of Ray Charles crooning "I Can't Stop Loving You." It was yet another defining moment in my life and began a love affair with music that has persisted to this day.

At night that summer, I discovered something on television far more sinister and terrifying than *The Huntley-Brinkley Report*—a show hosted by Boris Karloff entitled *Thriller*. It was an hour-long horror anthology series that featured writing by some of the finest authors of the time, including Robert E. Howard, Cornell Woolrich, Richard Matheson and Robert Bloch. The subject matter was of the ghastly and macabre variety and why my mother ever let me watch it is now hard to comprehend. In any case, I was completely and utterly captivated by *Thriller* and would always end up sleeping on the floor beside mom's bed later that night. I was too scared to be in my own room—even with my little sister sleeping there. Hell, I thought, she might not *be* my sister. She could be a warlock—and I just couldn't take that chance. But, like WHB did with music, *Thriller* cultivated a fascination within me for the horror genre that has endured through the years.

My little sister, it must now be noted, was not a warlock. She just sometimes acted like one.

Once the cast was removed from my foot, it was as if summer had finally begun—even though I had actually lost a month of it. An airless, stifling hot July had slowly covered the area like a tarpaulin. Mom couldn't afford to pay for us to go to the municipal swimming pool, so she usually found a friend to take us all to one of the many limestone quarries around the county. We would pack a picnic lunch and all sorts of inner tubes and vinyl rafts and head out for what would inevitably be an all-day affair—only heading for home when the stars begin to materialize in the purple twilight.

The cold quarry waters were a vivid, emerald green and mom always warned us that they were at least "60 feet deep." For me, that always conjured up images of a surfacing Loch Ness Monster or the Creature From the Black Lagoon. At the very least, perhaps a Spanish galleon was still resting on the bottom, festooned with rotting demi-culverins and teeming with precious gold and silver ingots.

I was careful, therefore, to keep my fingers and toes out of the water as my raft glided over the deepest part of the quarry. One never knew whether he might get snagged on a mast protruding just below the surface or capsized by a creature with fins and razor-sharp teeth.

All around, the cottonwoods were shedding their snow-like catkins and whispering with the help of a welcomed gentle south wind. The searing July sun reflected off the cool waters with a starburst effect. Dragonflies buzzed the scene and the voices of loved ones, happy and at play, filled the air. These were days to remember.

I learned not to get too complacent with the here and now, though.

Summer waned and soon we were to learn that mom was "looking for a house to rent." That timeworn, six-word phrase could mean only one thing—we were moving yet again. And this time not by choice. The nosy busybody last-known survivors of the Civil War who lived next door to our north had apparently had their fill of stumbling across the sidewalk littered with our toys and were tired of all the joyful noise emanating from our humble abode. After they met with the landlord, mom was given an eviction notice without any warning or grace period. We were out on our proverbial butts.

I was somewhat hopeful when I learned that when she finally found a suitable house, as opposed to an apartment, it was only about 10 blocks away on South Malcolm. Maybe, I thought, I would be able to stay and attend second grade at Roosevelt Grade School.

It was not to be, however, as we discovered that we would be in the zone for James B. Hutton Elementary School. Three different schools in three years. I felt like an Army brat minus the Army and its benefits. I don't really remember the move itself. It's as if it happened at night and in complete secrecy. All I knew is that our new house had a screened-in front porch and a large backyard with a garage/shed out by the alley.

I was also to get my own room. And just down the block a large wooded area beckoned. Kids seemed to be everywhere. The water treatment plant nearby offered possibilities for exploration. Hutton itself was very new compared to the redbrick, archaic structure that was Roosevelt. We would even have a new corner grocery store to shop at—Palen's Market.

Maybe this wasn't going to be so bad, I thought.

It was, after all, just another neighborhood.

THE WOODS, HOLIDAYS &
LIFE AT THE GULAG

IT WAS MERELY A THREE-ACRE tract of undeveloped land bounded on the west by South Ashby Avenue, on the east by South Katy Avenue, on the south by East 9ᵗʰ Street and on the north by sprawling, cavernous Elmwood Cemetery. After arriving at our rental house on Malcolm in Indian Summer 1962, one of the first things I discovered was this very large and topographically diverse playground that all of the neighborhood kids called simply "The Woods."

The west side was a dense thicket of Hickory and Wild Crabapple trees that ended abruptly at a small brook which meandered through woods from southwest to northeast. On the east side of the stream, a small, peaceful meadow faded into a tall grass ridge, which in turn melted into a smattering of Eastern Red Cedars and Mulberry bushes. As one might expect, this contradictory landscape became whatever kids were playing in it at the time wanted it to be—whether it was a distant planet, medieval forest or a dangerous jungle.

The Woods had an unparalleled capability of seemingly transforming itself with every season. It was wonderment to me how different it looked in the dead of winter, the trees stripped of their leaves and the ground covered in deep snow. Standing on the frozen stream and listening to the wind scream through the cedars, it was difficult to imagine that this was the same place where eight months earlier floodwaters from a spring thunderstorm transformed the flower-covered meadow into a churning lake.

Many a Pacific Theater battle was fought and won in those woods. Dragons were slain, Arctic expeditions launched and raids on Indian camps conducted amidst a backdrop of circling red-tailed hawks and croaking frogs. Naturally, though, we occasionally sought out even more dangerous and challenging adventures.

For that, all we had to do was cross Katy Avenue to the east. There, a monolithic and sinister looking Municipal Water Treatment plant loomed with dubious purpose. With its mysterious lagoons, filtration systems, sedimentation tanks and whirring pumps, the fortified complex immediately fell under our suspicion that it could be a Russian weapons-producing plant. Either that or I had seen *Dr. No* too many times.

In any case, we were never able to prove anything nefarious going on there. It did smell bad, though. Very bad.

Further to the east beyond the plant, the Missouri-Kansas-Texas railroad tracks separated us from the rest of the world. Occasionally we would wander to the edge of the tracks and wait for the southbound local hauling aggregates to trundle by. The line had become little-used, and coupled with Katy's reticence to upgrading its infrastructure, the tracks were uneven, causing the engine and gondola cars to lean precipitously and wobble back and forth. I can remember thinking of how mom was going to feel learning that her son had been crushed under the weight of tons of concrete that had fallen from a decrepit rail car. Hopefully, I thought, she will get a nice settlement from the MKT.

On the way home, we almost always walked the tracks down to 7th Street. Near the intersection of the street and rails was an old, dilapidated farmhouse where a large, black bull we called Jerry glowered behind a fence that looked suspiciously vulnerable. He would shuffle along the fence as we walked, snorting menacingly and slinging fluids. We were careful, of course, not to wear any red clothing lest he crash through the fence and attack us. I recall wondering how mom would have felt when the news reached her that I had been run down and fatally gored by an old bull on 7th Street. Unlike the MKT, there would be no monetary settlement from whoever owned the despairing farmhouse.

"If only he hadn't worn that shirt that had red stitching," she would have conjectured between sobs. Mom was a stickler for detail.

Many of these fun adventures came to an abrupt halt when classes at James B. Hutton Elementary School commenced after Labor Day Weekend. Days soon became filled with the intoxicating, imported and pungent aromas of purple mimeograph ink and Butch Wax, learning how to play "The Old Gray Goose Is Dead" on a fluteophone, climbing ropes in the gym, playing kickball and occasionally studying. The daily tedium inexorably, slowly settled into a tranquil numbness.

Then events far beyond my control flared up like solar fires, threatening to disrupt the gentle established rhythm. On a cold, drizzly night in late September at Comiskey Park in Chicago, brooding challenger Sonny Liston bludgeoned good-guy Floyd Patterson to the canvas in the very first round, separating him from both his senses and the Heavyweight Boxing crown. Norman Mailer would later comment that the fight was a "victory of sex over love." I knew sex was bad, and Liston looked like, at least on our grainy television set, a rabid pit bull with over-sized muscles. "This isn't good," I mused.

I barely had time to fully comprehend the Liston conquest, when three weeks later Huntley-Brinkley broke the news that an American U-2 reconnaissance spy plane had photographed missile bases being constructed with Russian assistance on the island of Cuba, just a hundred miles from mainland USA. This initiated a wrenching two week period in which Russia and the United States teetered on the brink of nuclear war. Everyday came new, grimmer updates and everyday came new questions. "Where will we hide when the bombs fly?"

All mom could do was look at us kids furtively and say "I don't know." Her answer, while brutally honest, was not very reassuring. I sought solace in The Woods, but there, too, was an undercurrent of fear among the creatures that only deepened my anxiety. Waiting for a nuclear blast can be very vexing.

Then, almost as quickly as it had begun, the Cuban Missile Crisis, as it later became known, was defused and ended. There was much celebrating, I can tell you now, in the Winslow house, when we learned that President Kennedy had successfully negotiated an end to the dangerous stalemate. In doing so, he transcended the office to become, in our eyes, a real life hero. We weren't going to die after all. At least not by the scorched heat of a nuclear fallout. I could now go back to worrying about wobbly train cars and agitated bulls behind rickety fences—and what to be for Halloween.

All Hallows Eve during those years on South Malcolm was, at least for us neighborhood ragamuffins, a cherished holiday. Every year the public school system held an art contest for grades K-6. The winner's drawings were displayed in downtown merchant's windows until the day after Halloween. It was very special to walk downtown, the blue-smoke air acrid with the smell of burning leaves, to try and find my poster.

The slow, steady march to Halloween actually started in late September with the annual Fall Festival Parade. Behind police cars with blaring sirens, area farmers would navigate their combines, balers and trucks down Main Street to the accompaniment of local bands. The Mexican Fiesta Queen and her attendants would smile and wave from convertibles loaned by Merle Kelly Ford, Ranz Motor Company and other dealerships. Cub Scouts, Girl Scouts and 4Hers tossed candy to the throngs lining the parade route. Mirza Shriners in their tasseled turbans weaved circles in their little miniature jalopies. Scary-looking clowns interacted with the crowd along the way.

The festivities continued into early October with the Biblesta Parade in nearby Humboldt, eight miles north of Chanute. Local churches, businesses, and organizations created floats for the parade based on Bible stories and themes. Additionally, there was almost always a Christian-music concert and bean-feed following the parade. I liked this parade very much because I never saw any scary-looking clowns there.

School activities in October included the anticipated chuck wagon chili supper and door-to-door U.N.I.C.E.F. panhandling drive. I always abhorred doing the U.N.I.C.E.F. collection because I was not very good at selling and also, just like the kids we were championing, we often didn't have enough to eat ourselves. I always felt like I should be going house to house for mom, not for a worldwide corporate organization. Boiled cabbage, navy beans and cottage cheese can only be served so many different ways before reality sets in.

The season culminated with a costume party/contest, Spook Parade down Main Street and then Halloween night itself. Just as soon as the sun set on that revered day, mom unleashed us on the city with our pillow cases for collecting candy. We would stay out until at least 9 or 10 PM canvassing as much territory as possible in the smoky, frosty night, jostling with spacemen, cowboys, werewolves, princesses and vampires.

Besides the normal store-bought candy, we collected a large portion of homemade treats such as caramel apples, popcorn balls, brownies, cookies and fudge. There was never a thought toward inspecting the sugary loot in those days—in fact most of the homemade goodies far surpassed the quality of the purchased kind. Some people, in lieu of candy, even gave out quarters. It is little surprise that I held Halloween up as the second most important holiday in kiddom. The most important holiday was only two months away.

Not even the annual Kiwanis Pancake Breakfast at the Masonic Lodge the first Saturday in November that launched the beginning of Pheasant hunting season in Kansas could keep my mind off the impending cherished season. As I sat wolfing down short stacks in the basement of the old, drafty brick building, I wondered when my time might come to partake of the proud Kansas heritage of hunting fowl. Without a dad, I knew my chances were remote at best. Still, I couldn't help but feel at ease among hunters garbed in orange and camouflage, the air reeking of maple syrup and coffee. Some day, perhaps, I thought, some day.

It was about this time that I actually started establishing friendships as opposed to hanging around with nameless rabble. Those kinds of things happen when you spend more than one year at a residence. Soon a symmetry evolved in my life, a peaceful sameness that was desperately welcomed.

The triumvirate of Halloween, Thanksgiving and Christmas holidays just might be the most special time of year for a kid growing up in a small town. Not only did it mean some serious time off from school, it was a time to get candy and presents—and eat turkey and pumpkin pie, too. For certain, there was no better time in my life as a kid than the 60 days between Halloween and the end of the year.

That tranquility was brutally interrupted, however briefly, on November 22, 1963. Hushed murmurs about President Kennedy being shot started circulating right after lunch on the playground. Then a PA announcement confirmed the awful truth—our Commander In Chief, the hero who had emerged from the Cuban Missile Crisis, our very own Camelot—was dead by an assassin's bullet in Dallas. School was immediately dismissed. Teachers and students alike exited the building visibly shaken.

I ran all of the way home that cold and cloudless day in a panic trying to assemble in my head what this might mean for my country, my town, my school and my family. It was almost too terrible to comprehend. Until, that is, I got home. Mom was sitting on the sofa, stricken and staring zombie-like at the TV set. The screen had started to roll, but she did not bother even to get up and adjust it. She had been crying and her eyes were still red and wet. "It's over," she whispered, almost to herself. "He's dead." I was looking for some reassurance that everything was going to be okay—that life would go on as before. All mom could do was shake her head and say, "It's over."

I went to my room, closed the door behind me, lay on the bed and wept, not really understanding why.

Life did go on, admittedly a little sadder than before, and slowly, sluggishly, things returned to normal. The countdown to Christmas had begun in full earnest that not even a State funeral could delay.

In those December days of milkweed cloudy skies and growling north winds, the walk to Hutton was short on distance but long on amazement and adventure. Starting out under a vermillion and apricot sunrise, my journey took me past familiar neighborhood homes— the Kirby's, the Storck's, the Ripples—and past The Woods where Cedar Waxwings now feasted on what few Mulberry bushes remained following the November gales. Their soft, whistled trills perforated an otherwise quiet dawn.

Hoarfrost glistened from the tall blades of grass and in the frozen ditches in the fronts of houses. Two blocks later and at the end of the trek, Hutton Elementary glowed like a jeweled oasis amidst a bleak backdrop of leafless trees and shingled rooftops.

"Hellooooo!" Ms. Hollenshead would announce sing-song as she bounded into our third grade classroom, a literal whirling dervish if ever there was one. She was the district music teacher responsible for the upcoming Christmas program, and making sure we were whipped into a veritable Yuletide frenzy was both her paid profession and her passion. We practiced and sang—even those of us unfortunates who couldn't hold a tune in a bucket—and practiced and sang with seemingly no end.

We were all equal in her eyes, if not her ears.

The program, just days away, launched the official beginning of Christmas vacation, which meant two weeks off from school. That made it the second most important USD 413 event of the year—

surpassed only by the annual picnic at Katy Park in May which was the official last day of classes.

After dark, downtown Chanute was literally abuzz with the bacchanalia of the season. Shoppers jostled and negotiated for position on the windswept sidewalks and in the department stores. The windows of nearly all Main Street merchants teemed with displays that featured such staples as manger scenes, elves, tinseled stars, stands of garland and bulbs of all colors. The line between secular and religious celebration seemed to blur as one at times.

A larger-than-life mechanical Santa Claus waved creepily at passersby from the J.C. Penney storefront window in the very heart of downtown. Inside, the wooden floor creaked and groaned under the increased pedestrian traffic. All of the ground floor cash registers had cables attached to them that extended up to the mezzanine. Any transaction that required change was wired up and then back down again. It was a unique, fascinating sight during the Christmas shopping season to see those cables whirring with commerce.

Now that the advancement to Christmas was in maximum overdrive, most of the stores began staying open late *every* night instead of just the usual Thursday nights. I especially remember badgering my weary mother to take us to Montgomery Wards, where the basement literally bubbled over with Schwinn bicycles, board games, toys and everything near and dear to an eight year old's heart. And at each Main Street intersection, from Evergreen in the east to Forest in the west, Christmas lights in the primary colors were strung from the four corner buildings to form a pyramid of light. The only thing missing, it seemed, was snow.

The Christmas tree that I longed for to grace our front window in that little grey-shingled house on Malcolm Street did not grow in the ground. It could be bought from a store or ordered out of a catalogue, though. We could not afford, mom reminded me, an aluminum tree with its accompanying color wheel that splashed green, red, orange and blue waves onto its branches that held white enamel balls with gold flecks. We couldn't even afford to buy a Douglas Fir or Scotch Pine at one of the many Christmas tree lots around town. No, our tree was the usual Red Cedar, culled from a friend's field, complete with birds nest and dormant spider webs. Still, by the time we had endowed it with our collection of hand-made and decrepit decorations, pulled from old boxes in the attic, I could forget about how arduous the task was getting it home, including the removal of the cedar gum from my hands—which often resisted soap and water. I loved the dusty, sweet and spicy smell loaned by the tree to the living room. Like wassail, it seeped into the very walls and often lingered long after the holidays had faded.

It was not unusual in those evenings of fuchsia sunsets, to hear and see carolers wandering through the neighborhood. "O Come O Come Emmanuel" never sounded as good as it did then, sung by shivering schoolmates and their doting parents, illuminated in the warm sheen of porch lights. They seemed to know every word without looking at a song book. The air, thick with the smell of burning wood being belched by chimneys up and down the block, was piercing, but the starless sky otherwise gave no hint of an approaching snow.

By the time the day of the Christmas program finally arrived, it was almost anti-climactic. So much energy and emotion had been poured into the preparation for the event that, coupled with the last day of school for two weeks, it almost seemed like an afterthought. Nevertheless, school dismissed for the day, and we all went to our homes to dress for the long-anticipated event. Later that evening, amidst a flotsam of parents, teachers, friends and relatives, we marched down the aisles of Memorial Auditorium. Dressed in our white gowns and carrying penlight flashlights, which supposedly symbolized candles, around our necks on a string, we followed Ms. Hollenshead's every lead. She was at her unflappable, legendary best that night and the crowd erupted with raucous applause after every song, no matter how off-key we sang. As we filed out of the auditorium and headed for home, I was certain that my young heart was richer for the experience.

Finally, the long, interminable wait for Christmas was nearly over. It did not snow that year, but on Christmas Eve, in the blue-violet of night, my sisters and I finally won a long-standing battle with mom and were allowed to open *one* present early. The one I chose consisted of a bag of WWII-era green plastic soldiers, whom I promptly pressed into service at the Battle of Stalingrad on the hardwood floor of my bedroom. Later that night, under heavy blankets, I lay quietly, trying to capture every sound yet wanting desperately for sleep to come so that the night would disappear and turn into morning.

I was up before sunrise that Christmas, in that enraptured hour between night and first blush, stealthily crawling like one of my plastic green infantrymen toward the living room. There, in the bewitched stillness, where the still-burning tree lights bathed the room in a rosy warmth and the floor furnace cracked and popped, evidence abounded that Santa had indeed come to our home. Stockings bulged with fruit, nuts, candy and toys. More presents had magically arrived underneath the Christmas tree. I huddled in the hushed silence and waited for the others to arise—spellbound by the magic that only December 25th could impart.

I did not get the electric NFL Football set that I so confidently sought that year. In fact, I don't even remember what the rest of my presents were—probably socks and homemade clothing. More important though, even at that early age, were the notions that family and love were the best gifts of all—and surely the most enduring.

The New Year ushered in bone-chilling, water pipe-freezing cold and the resumption of the academic gulag known as second semester. The only real thing to look forward to at that point was Valentine's Day, which most of us boys looked upon as lame and unnecessary. At school we 'traded' valentine's cards, so I was always looking for hidden or cryptic messages in my cards that confirmed my suspicion that Dee Dee Blake had a major crush on me—or that Lester Hoertz was actually an alien from a distant planet. After all, what could be gleaned from getting a valentine candy heart that said "Small Talk," "That Smile" or "I Wonder?" I wonder what? What the hell did that mean? I *wonder* if the candy-makers could be any more ambiguous?

I would have much preferred more direct messages on my candy hearts, such as "Dashed Hopes," "Wash Your Hair," "Cooties" or "You Suck at Dodge Ball." Palen's Grocery did not carry that type of valentine's candy, though—fortunately for me, I suppose.

School and life trudged along like an arctic glacier until about Easter, when we could finally see the light at the end of the tunnel. Once all of the boiled eggs were eaten and the painted Easter chicks had died one by one, the only thing left to ponder was the end-of-school picnic and field trip to Katy Park. All over town, trees began budding and shrubs and flowers burst forth with livid, fragrant colors. Even the last-gasp dusting of an early April snow could not dampen our enthusiasm for spring and what lie ahead.

The end of the school year was actually a series of events, preparatory in nature, which led to the doorstep of summer. The all-school P.E. Day (Physical Education Day) at old Royster Stadium was a time to pit school against school in various events and races. It was also a time to check out the girls from the other schools that we would eventually see in Junior High in a couple of years. Nothing, I had already learned, took the place of proper planning.

The field trip to Katy Park for us Huttonians was the *absolute* end of the dreaded academic year. We all brought sack lunches, played games and terrorized the inhabitants of Monkey Island. Then we all went home to contemplate three months without homework and teachers.

All was right in my world.

AT LONG LAST SUMMER

HAD THE STANDARD CALENDAR OR clock never been invented—or even if they had and there was simply no access to them in Chanute, Kansas in 1964—everyone knew the very moment when summer arrived. Especially those of us recently freed from the gaping maw of educational hell. And I was at ground zero of it all.

Directly north and right next door to our house was a small white clapboard home probably no more than one thousand square feet in size. Nine months out of the year the house sat dark and silent. Every year, sometime in late May, however, a very large old station wagon ambled up the driveway, spilling the Maring family out for the summer.

The Marings were Keith and Norma along with their four sons—Stan, Steve, Scott and Ron. They actually lived and worked in Lexington, Missouri, but every summer since 1956, when they accepted the position of City of Chanute Municipal Swimming Pool managers, the Marings caravanned to the tiny bungalow next door in what would eventually be a pilgrimage that would last 50 years.

Like the Cliff Swallows returning to San Juan Capistrano annually, the arrival of the Marings in Chanute *was* the official start of summer.

Kool-Aid stands, another harbinger of the season, popped up like dandelions all over the neighborhood, setting off fierce, sometimes brutal competition and price wars. Nothing beat spending a hot afternoon in the hushed, air-conditioned lobby of Zip Drug sipping on a Root Beer float and rummaging through the comic book rack—

even without Jackie. The Peter Pan Ice Cream stores were yet another summer favorite and a frequent destination.

Sometimes when things got too frantic around the house—which was often—or when I just wanted to be alone, I would head into The Woods. Most of these trips were at sunset or in the deepest plum of evening. I would find a comfortable spot in the meadow within earshot of the gurgling brook and lie down and gaze at the sky. A million fireflies fluttered about me, borne on warming, soft, south winds.

I especially enjoyed being there any time thunderstorms were imminent and forecast by Earl Ludlum. He was rarely wrong. There was little to compare with sitting in the meadow and watching the massive, billowing thunderheads building and rising like giant mushroom clouds. Lightning gashed the sky and thunder rattled through the neighborhood, sending all of the residents and The Woods creatures scurrying for cover. Not me, however. I always considered it a free audio and visual show courtesy of Mother Nature.

Once I was financially able to scrape up enough money to buy a dependable used bicycle, there really wasn't anywhere that I couldn't go in the city—as long as I didn't mind pedaling to get there. Mine wasn't so much of a used bicycle as *integrated parts* of other used bicycles. A set of butterfly handlebars here, a refurbished banana seat there, two of the baldest tires I had ever seen—and well, you get the point. She wasn't going to win any beauty contests.

With my newfound mobility, however, I soon discovered a whole new world—one that stretched beyond the boundaries of my little neighborhood. It didn't take long, for instance, to determine that the coldest bottle of pop could be found in a chest-type machine at the Mobil gas station down on West Main. The bottles hung by their necks in even rows in a refrigerated box that was so cold that the Double Cola brand that I favored often had the appearance of a brown slush. The carbonation when conjoined with the bitter cold of the soda made for an experience both frightening and exhilarative.

I suffered from headaches so intense that my hair hurt and eyes watered. On the other hand, I have never drunk anything remotely close to that heavenly elixir. Go figure.

Another favorite pastime was to watch the comings and goings of people on the move at the local bus and train depots. There, I witnessed countless ecstatic welcomes and tearful goodbyes—from young men on their way to boot camp waving out the Greyhound window at distraught parents to the weary, homebound businessman suddenly beaming at the sight of his family eagerly waiting on the train platform. The whole spectrum of human emotions were all there to absorb and experience, if only vicariously, at those two mortar and stone buildings.

The city's annual 4th of July fireworks display was held that year in the sprawling, vacant field between the swimming pool and the MKT railroad tracks. The view from blankets spread out on the cool grass high on a ridge near the pool was spectacular. So, too, was the pervading smell of Off, the high-powered insect repellent, and gunpowder of spent Black Cat firecrackers. In contrast to the auditory barrage of screaming rockets and cannonball detonations, I could hear, in between launches, the lows of cattle as they shifted nervously in their stalls at the livestock auction complex just downwind a few blocks. It was a pleasant contradiction of sorts.

On the rare occasion that mom could find someone brave enough (or foolish enough if I am to be honest at this point) to ferry us all out to the local drive-in movie, a memorable time was sure to be had. It didn't matter that the movies shown (twin-bills with a cartoon sandwiched in between) were several years old and had already enjoyed a full run in larger cities. It wasn't important that many of the hanging post speakers didn't work very well—if at all. So what if the PIC mosquito repellent coils that we had to ignite and set on the dashboard filled the car with mephitic, green smoke? Who cared if the hot dogs from the snack bar were served on stale buns and probably contained cow's lips and tongues? We were at the Neo-Cha Drive-in movie theater watching movies in a car and nothing could rain on our parade. Except for rain, maybe.

From the opening credits under a soft, gray twilight to the end of the night when theater ushers waved us out safely onto the highway with flashlights, our clothes reeking of PIC, the drive-in movies offered us a welcome diversion from the ordinary. Plus it meant getting to stay up past midnight.

At some point in time every summer, one of the many traveling carnivals would slide into town and set up shop north of the drainage canal in City Park. And for those of us who could not afford the privilege of traveling to Fairyland Amusement Park in Kansas City or Joyland Park in Wichita, the arrival of these itinerant gypsies was a pleasing sight. A challenging sight, as well, as enough pop bottles had to be found and sold, at two cents each, in order to be able to pay for the privilege to ride the Ferris Wheel and be terrified by the Tilt-O-Whirl, not to mention stumble down the darkened labyrinths of the Fun House.

More exciting than the rides was the always-tawdry "Science Gone Wrong" canvas tent, under which many odd and strange animal (and some human) deviations were presented—all for a quarter. It was both abhorrent and fascinating to view the menagerie of abnormalities on display—two-headed snakes, a calf with five legs and a pig with one eye to name just a few. Never mind that some of my buddies assured me that these were "fakes" and not genetically engineered. These were things they didn't show us in school, that's for sure.

My friends and I soon learned that the best time to go the carnival was on the Saturday right before they left town. For some reason, ticket prices were discounted greatly and we could always get more bang for our buck. All that was left come Sunday morning was a trash-strewn lot and memories of a pickled punk that I couldn't quite get out of my head.

Perhaps the most bizarre—not to mention dangerous—ritual of those summers on Malcolm Street was running after the City fogger machine. As part of the community's mosquito abatement program, at the onset of warmer weather a tractor pulling a trailer with a fog machine spewing what we now know was DDT would trundle down the streets. Gradually, groups of us kids would gather and run behind the cloud of blue-gray insecticide, laughing and playing—completely oblivious to the potential hazards. All we knew was that the smell wasn't unpleasant and we didn't have to worry about those pesky mosquitoes or flies for a while.

Baseball is summer's sport. In some ways, it is the definition of summer itself. Mom couldn't afford the fees for me to join any of the little league baseball teams in the city, so I never played an inning during my youth. I had dreams, to be sure, and they were fed by visits to Katy Field, where semi-pro teams would battle it out under the soft glow of lights. When they were not playing, the local Knights of Columbus sponsored a very good fast-pitch softball team that was quite competitive. I would walk home alone those nights after all of the lights had been extinguished and re-play the game—diving for line drives, stealing second base, whiffing the heavy hitter with a brutal slider. It was all good.

One of the most anticipated events of the summer was our trip to Wichita to visit my Aunt Beatrice and Uncle Marlon and my two cousins, Janey and Sherry Anne. My uncle was a white-collar Boeing employee and they lived in a very nice brick rancher on Pawnee. It was air conditioned and had a sprawling, cool basement full of games and toys, including a ping pong table. Basically, they had everything we didn't. I was never jealous or envious of that, though—just grateful that I could spend one week every summer with them. Other than the trip to Indiana in 1958, Wichita was the farthest I would travel until much later in my life.

To get us there required some sacrifice on my aunt and uncle's part. As we didn't have a car, they had to drive 113 miles one way to pick us up, take us to Wichita, return us back and then drive home. All of it was accomplished in a 1959 Pontiac Kingswood Safari Station Wagon that seated about 30 people. I had never seen anything like it. Actually, it was more than a car. It was closer to a half-track on the family tree of vehicles. The only thing that saved it from being misidentified as a military vehicle was its color—white, with red interior.

The coolest thing about it, though, had to be the seat next to the tailgate. It was designed with an option to face *backwards*. I can't properly describe to you how exhilarating it was to set in the air-conditioned comfort of that cardinal red seat and see the Flint Hills roll by *backwards*. Suffice it to say that you had to get to the car first to secure that luxury. I learned to be cat-like quick.

The caravan to their home took us west across Kansas Highway 96, an incredibly dangerous and narrow ribbon of two-lane terror through the southern Flint Hills, ages-old rolling grasslands formed by the erosion of Permian-age lime stones and shales. While the scenery was quite striking and beautiful, there were no shoulders on the road and very few places to turn out and fix any kind of mechanical problem or flat tire that might befall a brave traveler. There were only a couple of gas stations and cafes open on the entire hundred-plus mile trek. And they looked like relics of the 40's or 50's manned by Ma and Pa Kettle.

So the excitement was rivaled only by white-hot fear—especially when we drove it at night.

I am happy to report that we always made it there and back safely—and in one piece—so kudos go to Uncle Marlon for not only keeping us out of harm's way, but also for the thousands of gallons of gasoline that it took for the journeys. Time spent at my cousin's always flew by as if on a jet stream. Especially when we all went to picnic at Riverside Park, just south of downtown Wichita on the banks of the Arkansas River. They had the coolest, baddest swings I had ever seen. I could get up so high that I could almost pick leaves off of the cottonwoods and bring them back down to earth.

Days were spent playing in the basement, discovering previously unknown things such as a mall and hanging out with all of my cousin's neighborhood buddies—the Avilas and the Bakers. Wichita might as well have been New York City in my eyes—I had never been anywhere where the tallest building was higher than six stories. It was all very fascinating and invigorating.

There were four-lane highways, clover leafs and a maelstrom of traffic that made Chanute look like the small town it really was.

Being the "air capital of the world," the skies above Wichita in those years rumbled with the thunder of commercial and military aircraft, adding to the mystique and fun.

Needless to say, the drive back was almost always fused with melancholy and the sad realization that summer was waning. Not to mention we all had to go back to a house with no air conditioning. The tearful goodbyes that I had previously only witnessed at the depots now became my own personal angst as I watched the big, white station wagon pull away from the curb on south Malcolm.

Days later, the USS Maddox, a Navy Destroyer, engaged three North Vietnamese P-4 Torpedo Boats while on patrol in the Gulf of Tonkin, a body of water half a world away in Southeast Asia. The incident would lead to an escalation of American involvement in the area and eventually lead to the undeclared Vietnam War. I wondered secretly if Uncle Marlon's venerable old station wagon might be pressed into service as a gunboat. If so, I wanted dibs on the back seat.

If it hadn't been for the boundless generosity of the Marings, I am not sure if summer could have been salvaged after the Wichita trip. Norma, the stoic and indefatigable lifeguard with sun-bleached hair, and Keith, the paratrooper who served under Patton—turned math instructor, had a knack for looking the other way or forgetting to always charge us for admission to the swimming pool. The remainder of the season meant spending whole days there only to return home with prune-like skin reeking of Coppertone and eyes burned red from the chlorine.

Soon, though, the cicadas would begin to conduct their symphonies earlier in the evenings. The baseball diamonds would be raked and laid idle. The swimming pool would be drained and the Marings would pack up their belongings and return to their "other" home for the winter. Another school year was approaching fast.

At the very end of that summer, a curious event occurred. My father showed up unannounced for a visit—much to mom's chagrin. My recall of certain specifics of that day are not very good, but I do remember that he took me for a ride in his new car and he bought me a baseball, glove and bat. I thought it was ironic that he would purchase for me a gift that was too late for the season to enjoy and not much use when we couldn't afford the entry fees to play in the first place. Still, I was happy just to be in his company—it really didn't matter if he bought me anything at all.

For some reason, my sisters did not take part in his visit—it was just the two of us, father and son. We spent the whole day together driving around town, talking and laughing. It was like he had never gone away. Time breezed by and I didn't want it to end.

Soon enough, though, we were back at the house on South Malcolm and he was hugging me tightly on the sidewalk. Looking down at the ground so he couldn't see my chin quiver, I remember noticing the wide cracks in some of the bricks through eyes heavy with tears. "I will be back again soon," he promised. "In the meantime you take care of yourself."

I nodded my head in response and without a further word, he walked stoically to the car and waved goodbye. Soon the Chevy—and my father—were both out of sight.

I would not see him again for 41 years.

Summer was over.

RUNNING WITH THE PACK

BY THE START OF THE 1965 school year, Winston Churchill and Malcolm X, heroes on opposite ends of the spectrum, were both cold in their graves and the anti-war movement was growing parallel with our ever-burgeoning involvement in Vietnam. Strategic bombing of North Vietnam commenced in March of that year in a move that was intended to degrade the enemy's air defense systems and industrial infrastructure. I began fifth grade at the Hutton Elementary School rock pile.

Immediately, things started to tilt toward the surreal—a sure sign of trouble to come. One prematurely cold, starless night in late September, a knock came upon our door from a neighbor down the street. "The Woods are on fire," he exclaimed in a panic before disappearing off into the darkness. I was the only one in the house that night to respond, and grabbing my jacket, flew out the front door with certain nervous dread.

The sky to the direct east of our backyard and alley glowed with a deep orange and there was an accompanying roar to the tableau that immediately signaled to me that this was no small incident. Arriving on the scene to find many other concerned neighborhood kids and parents, it was obvious that the conflagration was past the point of no return. Some of my buddies were throwing dirt and rocks on the fire, but with flames at the center knifing ten to twenty feet high, it was a hopeless, futile gesture.

Rumors swirled through the crowd like the tendrils of smoke that now drifted over Elmwood Cemetery on the heels of a harsh, cold north wind. Arsonists were to blame. It was an accidental fire started by one of the neighborhood regulars playing with matches. The truth was somewhat more painful, however; developers were preparing the land for future construction. That explained the bulldozers, fire department personnel and equipment that had gathered on 9th Street at the north entrance to The Woods.

I left the scene to return home that night with the funereal knowledge that I would never again be able to catch tadpoles from the lazy brook, nor would I ever be able to lay in the meadow and watch Mother Nature's light show roll in from the west. Future wars and Indian raids would have to be conducted from some other vantage point. Hawks and rabbits would be pressed to find new homes and hunting grounds. Later that night I lay in bed but refused to cry— though the loss was tangible, as if my stomach had been torn out and thrown in the fire. An icon of my childhood—perhaps the first real playground of my life—was gone and there was nothing I could do to save it or even bring it back.

It didn't really hit me, though, until the walk to school the following morning. I purposely avoided trekking past The Woods and instead headed north up the alley between Malcolm and Ashby Streets. As I crossed 9th Street, however, I glanced to the east and caught a glimpse of reality. A few skeletal, black and smoldering trees were still standing, though the rest of The Woods had been rendered unrecognizable. Bulldozers were already plowing through the north end and the air was laden with a sooty finality. It was one of the few times in my life that the bell to begin class would be a welcome respite—a chance to forget, if only temporarily, what had been done to a favorite, magical place.

When not doing homework in the evenings, I developed a new favorite pastime—perusing the various music and variety shows on network TV. My favorites included *Hullabaloo* with its caged "go-go girls," and *Shindig!* which showcased such musicians as The Animals, Beau Brummels and Petula Clark. *Shindig!* also featured their very own dance troupe that called themselves "the shin-diggers."

Of course, the bellwether of all televised music shows in 1965 was *American Bandstand*, and I watched with an unwavering intensity. Dick Clark was ultra-cool and all of the kids were well-dressed, cute and unnaturally hip. They rated music and counted down the top ten.

Outside of *The Munsters* and *The Man From U.N.C.L.E.*, there wasn't a better show on television at the time.

This was a unique time in televised medium history where gaps in network scheduling allowed, required actually, local programmers to come up with their own shows. One of those creations that arose from the ether on KODE-TV, our ABC affiliate, was a dance show in the same vein as *American Bandstand* called *Teen Hop*. It was a poor man's *American Bandstand* to be sure. Host Roger Neer was affable but without the imperturbable persona of Dick Clark. The kids, all from area high schools, appeared stiff and nervous as they danced for $25.00 grand prize money and all of the Kitty Clover Potato Chips they could scarf down. *Teen Hop*, short-lived as it was, gave hope to all of us small-town kids that we could have an *American Bandstand* experience—and only have to drive to Joplin to get it.

On October 2nd we attended the annual Biblesta Parade in Humboldt. The sky was heavy and gray but belied the unusually warm temperature. I first began to feel ill during the parade and got demonstrably worse on the eight mile ride home—sweating profusely and shaking with the chills. It was a very strange feeling and I knew that something was seriously wrong with me.

Once back in Chanute, we stopped by my mom's friend Bonita's house—she had let us ride with her to the parade as we had no car—to visit with her two daughters. I declined to go in as I was feeling worse and instead lay down in the back seat of her car and went to sleep. When I awoke it was morning and I was a patient at Neosho Memorial Hospital.

Admitted unconscious the night before with a dangerous body temperature of 106F, I was given a hypo and placed in IC with a case of acute pneumonia. It was impressed upon me that I was lucky to have survived such a prolonged period of elevated temperature. I would spend one week in the new Pediatrics wing of the hospital recovering slowly and reading get well wishes from fellow Hutton prisoners. I also got my picture shot by and published in the *Chanute Tribune* as the first patient in the new children's wing.

It was an odd experience in that I was taken to the play area, where I had never actually spent any time, and the photographer and attending nurse posed my by some building blocks for the money shot. I knew immediately that there would be some explaining to do back at school when the kids saw my picture in the paper that showed me appearing to be playing with toys clearly better suited for a 4 or 5 year old. Worse yet, the caption under the photograph as it was published listed me as the "son of Mrs. Burl Winslow." There was no mention of my father. It was if he were dead. Or never existed.

Other than making a full recovery and not having to go to school for five days, the only other positive that would come of my weeklong stay at the hospital was the discovery of a book that would launch me headfirst into a love of writing that would culminate with the memoir that you are now reading. The book was entitled "Norman The Doorman," by Don Freeman about a mouse who lives in the basement of an art museum and acts as a doorman for all of the other creatures who wish to see the treasures stored there. I was enthralled and knew exactly what I wanted to do with my life—write and illustrate children's books.

Those ambitions would have to wait until I graduated from college—at least twelve long years in the future, though, and the road there would take some very interesting turns. The first of which came after Thanksgiving of 1965. Mom announced that we would be moving yet again. The new house was located on West Walnut in the north part of town. Alcott Elementary School would be my new educational fortress after the Christmas break. Changing schools was bad enough, but to do so in the middle of the year was unconscionable in my view.

It was always a puzzlement to me as to why we kept moving—I never knew whether mom just got bored staying in one place too long, if she had a spat with the landlord or if she was merely trying to stay one step ahead of creditor wolves. Whatever the reasons were, she never shared them with us kids. We were left to say goodbye to buddies and school chums as well as the daunting task of making new friends. It was a growing feeling of impermanence, though, that stung the most and left the biggest psychological scar.

That Christmas season was a paradox of emotions. Joy that the holidays typically elicited was tinged with the sadness that separation induces. It culminated on a windswept, cold and snowy day in mid-December with a knock on the front door. There, volunteers from the local Veterans of Foreign Wars, made aware of our always-in-need condition, came clomping into the house, kicking slush from their boots and carrying boxes and bags of foodstuffs. I didn't know whether to laugh or cry—whether I should be grateful for the kindness of strangers or embarrassed that we were in that condition in the first place.

I decided right there and then that, when I became an adult, I would never put myself or my family in a position where we counted on the generosity of others for survival.

Never.

The holidays came and went and in January 1966 we moved into the very large, two-story clapboard home on Walnut. I was struck immediately by how *huge* it was compared to the other houses we had lived in previously. We didn't even have enough furniture to fill it up. It even had a garage for the car we didn't own. The bedrooms, both of them, were on the second floor and cavernous. Mom appointed those rooms to us kids while she transformed the formal dining room on the first floor into her bedroom. It was by far the nicest and roomiest house we had ever lived in—there was just one problem, and it was a big one—Periplaneta Americana—better known as the American Cockroach.

None of us had ever dealt with roaches before, but it was clear right from the start that this was no small insect problem. Like the North Vietnamese regulars, they just kept coming and coming. Nothing we did ever blunted their invasion. At night the walls in the kitchen turned brown with them. There were so many of them that you could *hear* them as they skittered about.

They would fall on us from the ceiling, crawl across us as we slept at night and lay eggs on our clothes in our dresser drawers. Because of the massive infestation, I vowed, if ever I made friends in the new neighborhood, to never bring them over to play at my house.

I did make new friends, though, and right away. One of them was a former classmate at Hutton named Darren Kelly. How he was able to live a few houses down from us yet still attend school at Hutton instead of Alcott was apparently a trick my mom hadn't picked up on. His dad was a baker who liked to imbibe a little when he wasn't mass-producing Bavarian Crème doughnuts at his downtown shop.

His mom was a petite housewife who could cook up a storm and was never seen nor photographed without a cigarette dangling from her lips. Darren was the youngest of the three Kelly kids. He had a bowl haircut and could run very fast. He introduced me to Jerome Baker, a friend of his who attended the Catholic Church school.

Jerome and I hit it off immediately and had much more in common. He lived with his mom because his parents divorced. He rarely saw his dad and he was an avid reader and basketball player. He used to play Darren *and* me in 2-on-1 and Horse and we never beat him. Ever. His record against us was approximately 175-0. We rarely *scored* on him either.

As the school year progressed onward, I met and befriended Charles Greene, a big, muscular 12 year old who had been held back one year. He was tall and had a mop of curly blond hair. It was likely that he may have actually been older than 12 because I think he was already shaving by the Spring of 1966. He beat up other kids on a regular basis for making fun of his cleft lip and palate. I made sure to never call him "hair-lip." That set him off in a frenzy that often resulted in someone taking a first class beat-down.

Charles was the one who introduced me to Suicide Hill, and I will forever be in his debt for that. Suicide Hill was an aptly named slope of tall grass on the southeast quadrant of the K-39 overpass at the eastern edge of the city. Like a P.E. might lecture his students about the thermal dynamics of refrigeration and the importance of enthalpy charts, Charles would hold court with us lesser men about the do's and don'ts of surfing Suicide Hill in flattened cardboard boxes.

For instance, one must wait, he cautioned, until the grass had died in the fall and was sufficiently brittle before doing any surfing. The more dead and dry the grass, for instance, the faster the descent. Never surf in the morning or evening as moisture becomes a slowing factor. He would even provide elaborate discourse on the types of boxes best suited for the task. Those with wax finishes were a definite no-no and should be left in the dumpster.

My inaugural trip down Suicide Hill was in the Autumn of 1966 and it was with Dr. Greene as my driver and confidante. We pushed off on an old washing machine box from the highest point of the slope, which appeared to be just under the lowest deck of clouds in the sky. With speeds of up to 150 MPH, we streaked down the embankment toward certain death. Then, about halfway down, we hit a small bump in the terrain, which at a normal pace would have had little or no impact. Sailing across it at warp speed, though, produced the effect of launching us into the air, then falling back to earth like space junk re-entering the stratosphere, crashing into the ravine at the end of the slope with arms and legs twisted and turned in ways that were not altogether normal. It was the most exhilarating thing I had ever done in my young life.

And that included stepping off the 15-foot high diving plank at the swimming pool and riding the Tilt-A-Whirl, with its creepy clown face stenciled on the back of the ride, at the carnival.

Suicide Hill would become an integral part of my childhood from that point forward, but it would have to be shared with other new discoveries that came fast and furious. In the dead of Winter 1966, for instance, we decided that it was time to scale the old city water tower in Highland Park. Like Robert Peary's conquest of the North Pole in 1909, climbing the imposing 60-foot tower, with its frozen metal ladder and rickety railings, was a dangerous, if not foolhardy gamble.

While we didn't plant a flag at the summit, Charles and I spray-painted our initials on one side of the vessel. The view from the lofty perch was, to put it succinctly, breathtaking. Rooftops—even treetops—dwarfed below us and cars and trucks took on the appearance of miniature models. To this day, I can't really explain what propels many young males to seek to climb trees, water towers, house roofs, etc., but I can say with certain authority that there is a feeling of *transcendence* with being above everyone else. To share space with birds and clouds is like no other experience. The fact that it was illegal to climb the tower in the first place made it that much more appealing to us.

The trick, I soon learned, in not getting caught was to get up and down the vertical ladder as fast as possible. Once you were at the top, there was little chance that anyone on the ground would look up and spot you. Like Suicide Hill, we became regular visitors to the Highland Park water tower as well as the other two towers in town. And we never got caught.

Charles was also solely responsible for introducing me to a game that I quickly figured out was one of his making. The game was called "The Bird" and it involved, quite simply, going downtown to any street corner and watching as the older teenagers and twenty-something's "drag" Main. Once there for a short time, we identified a "target" vehicle and as it passed by us we gave them the middle finger salute, or "the bird."

Naturally, this caused an immediate, convulsive and violent reaction to all of the inhabitants of said vehicle. A typical response had them either slamming on their brakes and everybody but the driver bailing out and giving chase or racing around the block to try and cut us off. In either case, however, it was futile as we knew every alley and doorway, every ladder and rooftop in all of downtown Chanute. It was both horrifying and extremely gratifying to watch from the apex of a downtown building as hordes of angry teenagers canvassed the area looking for their tormentors.

It was about that time that I began to identify Charles with activities that involved the chance of bodily harm. Suicide Hill, climbing water towers and giving older, bigger and faster kids the middle finger were definitely enterprises where we stared the possibility of an extended hospital stay right in the face. I could only wonder what he would want to do next—fabricate homemade bombs in the basement of his home or dive off the east river bridge to see how deep the water was.

In any event, it was sure to be a surreal time with the big kid whose idea of fun was peeing in the floor furnace of his house and then watching as his parents vainly tried to figure out what the strange stench was. He was cut from a different cloth, that's for sure.

In February of 1967, Jerome asked Darren and I to help him a couple of days a week after school on his paper route in north Chanute. He was a delivery boy for the *Chanute Tribune*, and he needed help throwing papers and collecting the money. His territory ran from Steuben and Main all the way north to the end of the city limits. I don't know how he did it all after school by himself and still got home before midnight.

We agreed to help him as it allowed us all more time together plus he shared his take with us. It was my introduction into the world of profit-sharing.

Little did we know how truly unappreciated the life of a newspaper delivery boy was. Meeting at the *Tribune* office to pick up the papers would prove to be the highlight of the day. It all went downhill from there. The *Tribune* was a phantasmagorical place chock full of strange sights, sounds and smells—churning presses, overpowering aroma of inks and all levels of people moving frantically about in the quest to make seemingly impossible deadlines. I loved it.

For starters, the paper had to be folded in a manner not unlike that of an American flag when it comes down from a pole or is presented in a formal ceremony. This was, Jerome explained, done to allow the paper to be thrown like a Wham-O Frisbee from the street to the front porch of houses. It helped to expedite the time it took to work both sides of Steuben Street for the mile and a half journey.

Naturally, all of the papers that I had folded came apart at some point during the airborne sequence. This caused me to have to pick the paper up—usually out of a hedge or bush or in some cases a mean dog's fenced-in home—and re-fold it and place it on the porch. In worst-case scenarios the paper simply and literally came unraveled during flight and pages and inserts alike took to the wind, ending up in trees and on rooftops or blowing down the street never to be seen again. Luckily, Jerome always packed extra papers.

Following an afternoon of running from unchained, rabid dogs and neighborhood bullies—and trying to pry subscription money from skinflint customers—there was a reward of sorts at the end of the route. If, and if is the proverbial word here, we were able to generate any kind of revenue from collections, Jerome set aside all that was due to the *Tribune* and split the rest between us. That usually meant a trip to Disney's Market on North Santa Fe where we would blow it all on cold pop and candy.

Sometimes, we rode our bikes all the way down to Barker's for an evening of chili cones, vanilla Cokes and pinball.

If we didn't make the necessary collections, which happened from time to time, an optional plan was exercised—a plan that might have caused me to be banished to Hades in the afterlife. On those occasions where we were left broke—or nearly broke—and meandering the streets home with empty paper bags, we sometimes stopped by Old's Grocery at the corner of 5th and North Grant Streets. There, a diminutive elderly widower, Mrs. Old, lorded over her decaying mercantile with a kindly benevolence.

This was the quintessential corner mom-and-pop grocery store. Mrs. Old even lived in the rear of the place.

Our ruse was a simple one—one of us, usually me because of my gift of gab—would wander around to the back of the store to knock on Mrs. Old's personal door. As it usually took her about 10 minutes to shuffle from behind the cash register and counter to the back door, Jerome and Darren would then quietly enter the front door. While I engaged Mrs. Old in some rudimentary conversation, they would, with silent efficiency, stuff our empty paper bags with Cherry Mashes, Val-O-Milks, Jawbreakers, Potato Chips, etc.

At this point I would like to reassure the reader that we never cleaned her out, nor did we ever steal any money from the cash register. And *I* never personally stole anything from her. I was merely a diversionary accomplice. Guilty by association at the very most.

That doesn't take away from the fact that it was wrong, though. By the time I had grown up and was somewhat wiser, it was too late to repent to Mrs. Old. She was long gone. So, if you are up in Heaven, Mrs. Old, and looking down, please accept my sincere and most humble apologies. We were just kids struggling to find our way—and there is no justifiable excuse for what we did.

I have since tied my misdeeds at Old's Grocery to Karma. For instance, immediately after our first heist, our family cat, Mimi, an exquisite and beautiful Calico, was run over by a car right in front of our house. To make matters worse, she was pregnant. All of us were mortified at the sight. I was sure that it had everything to do with our crime.

Fate finally caught up with me on a humid, rainy Sunday afternoon in April 1967. I got caught trying to steal some felt tip pens from a local store downtown variety store. It was a humiliating experience for me, but devastating to my mom. This was a problem, she reminded me in the therapeutically cold light of the store manager's office, that she did not need to be dealing with. "I am raising my three children on my own," she sheepishly confided to the manager, "and I am trying to find a job."

The police were called, but the manager, seeing how repentant I was and perhaps sensing my mother's precarious situation, declined to press charges. A worse fate, I knew, awaited me at home. I got grounded for a month and was not allowed to hang out with any friends until school got out in May. I was also banned from watching television for two weeks, so no *Teen Hop* either.

The list of what I would be missing was a long one. No chili cones. No Suicide Hill. No water tower. No more running with the pack.

For the next month it would be just me, my miserable conscience, homework and the roaches. And perhaps the dire knowledge that the road to Hell was lined with stolen Val-O-Milks and Magic Markers.

THE ERIE CONNECTION

IN THE LATE SPRING AND early summer of 1967, a series of low pressure systems formed and barreled out of the four corners area where the borders of Utah, Colorado, Arizona and New Mexico intersect. As a result of this meteorological occurrence, a literal conveyor belt of thunderstorms was delivered to the southeastern corner of the state of Kansas. By late June, most of the region's major rivers and their tributaries of creeks, brooks and streams were out of their banks and spilling into the bottoms and lowland areas. Eventually, as the rains persisted with a malevolent sameness, the turgid waters would creep into the rich, fertile farmlands of the region, hampering crop maintenance as well as delaying the annual wheat harvest. Sixteen years after the "flood of the ages," local residents began to wonder if it could all happen again. The worry was palpable—in the eyes and on the craggy, furrowed brows of everyday people.

Sixth grade graduation from Alcott Elementary School brought on a predictable dichotomy of emotions. While I was elated that the 7-year prison sentence was finally over, I was nervous about a number of new, looming unknowns. Junior High was a big step and I wondered how I would cope at a place where all of Chanute's grade schoolers came together for the first time. What kind of hazing ritual would we have to endure from the 9th graders there? We all knew that we would have classes in multiple rooms (and even multiple buildings) and that we HAD to take communal showers after gym class.

It didn't help that Mr. Owens, my revered 6th grade teacher, a wise and good-hearted instructor if ever there was one, warned us boys on the last day of school to "keep our socks dry." As innocuous as it sounded, I quickly identified his admonition as a pointed and undeniable reference to the raging conflict in Vietnam. I would be eighteen in just six short years. Surely the war would be over by then, I thought.

Alcott was barely in my Schwinn Stingray's rear-view mirror when my mother, perhaps sensing I was planning a summer of fun and sun with my friends, announced that I would be going to my maternal grandmother and Uncle Al's house in Erie, Kansas for a week. By myself. Now, at that point, I began to assess the most recent past in search of a reason, or reasons, that I was to be furloughed to this unfamiliar place whose inhabitants I barely knew.

Was it due to the shoplifting incident at Gibson's Discount Center the previous April? No, that couldn't be it, as I had tearfully repented for my crime and charges were dropped by the kindly store manager. Was it because of all of the C's I had accumulated on my grade card in Ms. Eastburn's morning class the second semester? No, that surely wasn't it, either, as I had quite a number of A's and B's from Mr. Owen's afternoon class to offset the moribund performance.

Was it because I resolutely hung on to my friendship with Jerome, my Catholic buddy, in the face of mounting opposition from both of our mothers? Knowing how much I loved to read, he had, during my house arrest, managed to smuggle a copy of George Orwell's "Animal Farm" to me. Mom had singled out Jerome for my recent bad behaviors, when in truth it was really my entire fault.

We were not aware, apparently, that even in a small community in the Midwest, Catholics and Protestants were dissuaded to mingle. Still, against all odds, we maintained our friendship. But, no, that wasn't the reason I was being sent to Erie. In the end, despite countless hours of retracing my steps over the last year, I couldn't come up with one good reason that I would be banished for a week.

I packed my suitcase as if I were heading toward the dreaded Boys Industrial School in Topeka—a place every boy (and some of the rougher girls, too) were threatened with by parents trying to keep us all on the "straight and narrow." Never mind that I didn't know one single person who got sent there or if the place even existed—the mere idea that *I* could end up there was enough to keep me running faster, climbing higher and doing whatever it took to *not* get caught and sent to this children's prison.

The sky was low and opaque and the air boiling on the Saturday morning when Mrs. Jenkins, my grandmother's case worker, pulled up into our driveway in her redoubtable midnight blue 1965 Dodge Polara. As she had to travel to Erie to meet with my grandmother to discuss her "case"—whatever that meant—she was pressed into double-duty service as my chauffer. Mrs. Jenkins was a kindly, older woman, bent over and stooped—seemingly not much younger than my grandmother herself. She had a way of engaging with people that made them feel very comfortable. Considering the journey I was about to embark upon, hers was just the right demeanor for the 16 mile ride to the unknown. No one came out to say 'goodbye' as we rumbled down the driveway and out onto Walnut Street. Perhaps it was just as well—I might have jumped out of the car if they had.

The ride to Erie took us east on Kansas Highway 96, where we crossed the Neosho River a few miles outside of town. It was then that the sudden reality of the flood jolted me in the air-conditioned comfort of my seat. As we crossed the steel truss bridge, I peered down into the foaming, turbulent brown waters that appeared to be but just a few feet from the deck. The normally peaceful river was a raging torrent, and had breached its eastern bank. Fields of new corn were now fully under water. It was a terrifying sight. As we passed over the approach, I began to worry whether I might not make it back in a week.

What would happen if the bridge were washed out? What if floodwaters crested the highway and traffic was halted? Would I have to live with my grandmother and Uncle Al in their little hovel for the summer? The thought made me shudder. Mrs. Jenkins, perhaps sensing my fear, offered that the forecast was for sunny weather in the coming week. I was not reassured, however, as we passed over Big Creek, Canville Creek and countless other feeders that seemed to be hopelessly high and ready to flow over their bridges at any moment.

It seemed like we had traveled for hours, but soon we reached the city limits of Erie, the county seat of Neosho County, Kansas. At that time there were about 1,500 residents there, one stoplight, and one general store—Duckwall's. There was no movie theater (it had burned to the ground in a recent fire,) but there was a modest, fairly new public swimming pool. The county courthouse was a modern blonde-brick structure that had replaced a dilapidated old redbrick one in 1960. Main Street was lined with old buildings with the dates of their origin engraved on their parapets. The Santa Fe and MKT Railroads intersected in town, and the local farmer's cooperative did steady, brisk business. This was a prototypical, calendar farming community full of modest, but well-cared for homes, verdant lawns, pretty churches and manicured parks. On the way to grandmother's house, we passed a little, rundown dairy bar on the east side of town. I wondered whether they might serve chili cones—the one thing that could possibly transform my week there from mind-numbing boredom to reluctant acceptance.

Soon we pulled up in front of the little shack at the corner of 7th and Massachusetts streets. I had been here a few times before—with other family members—but never for such an extended amount of time. My mother had had a frosty relationship with her mother for many years, and as a result, we did not spend much time at her house. Apparently, grandma Nellie was married numerous times and had so many children that it became imperative, in order to survive, that she ship some of them out to other relatives to care for. This, I came to understand, was not that unusual in depression-era America. It was unfortunate for my mother, though, that not only was she one of the children that was sent away, but that she was abused and neglected by her mean-spirited custodians. She left their home at age eighteen and to the best of my knowledge, never entirely forgave my grandmother for it.

Grandma Nellie doted on her Steinberg kids, though—of which, Uncle Al, who lived with her—was one. He was an unemployed 44 year old bachelor with pomaded black hair, baboon-like face and a penchant for "junking," making trips to the local dump and foraging for treasures—and swilling coffee at all three cafes in town. The results of his many forays to the landfill were in evidence everywhere in the backyard of the house. There were literally mountains of junk— discarded bicycles, washing machines, couches, farm implements, barrels, crates, kitchen utensils, toys, boards, tires—as far as the eye could see. Every square inch of the lot, it seemed, was usurped with a flotsam of clutter and someone else's debris.

Despite this, however, the front and sides of the property were a thing of beauty to behold. The lawn was expansive and flourishing—a beautiful, emerald green cut to perfection by grandma with a manual oscillating mower. There were Mock Orange bushes on the north side of the porch and Lilac's in full bloom on the south side of the yard near the drainage ditch. Iris's of various hues stood guard by the mailbox and sidewalk. Best of all, though, were the Honeysuckle's that grew right behind the swing on the front porch. My older sister told me how grandma Nellie would sit and swing with her in the tranquil summer evenings, singing softly, the air enchanted with the sweet perfume of the honeysuckle—and the yard sparkled by the light of a million fireflies.

All of it just beyond a mountain range of rubbish.

Mrs. Jenkins met with grandma Nellie for about twenty minutes and then was waving goodbye to me and trodding out of the yard towards her car. She was to return the following Sunday to get me for the trip home. As it was, according to Uncle Al, too late to hit the coffee shops and dump, he settled down to an afternoon of doodling and drawing. I soon learned that he was an accomplished artist—all of which is most unusual considering that he never had a formal art lesson in his life. He could sketch and paint nearly anything—and was particularly gifted when it came to human anatomy. Especially female anatomy. I had never seen anything quite like this. Soon, we were penciling sketches together and time literally flew by.

In the first evening of my week there, grandma and Uncle Al introduced me to a bevy of unusual neighbors. One of them was old Mr. Brazier, who lived across the street and talked with a corn-cob pipe clinched between his teeth. He left his front door open on warm evenings, and frequently you could hear the belly laughs he emitted from watching comedy shows on TV all the way down the street. Pudd and Ode were two aging black men who had survived some obviously rough times to retire in a little, cluttered home on South Massachusetts. They used to give my older sister money to go to the swimming pool when she visited grandma Nellie. They enjoyed sitting in their peeling metal lawn chairs and doling out scraps of food to Mickey, my grandma's beloved Heinz 57 dog.

Florence Mose, one of the few people that grandma called "friend," had a crooked walk and an unusual lisp. Words that ended with Y or IE would somehow end up with a K attached to them in her world. Therefore, my grandma Nellie was always "Nellick" to Florence. There was a sign-painter who lived down the block that could always be found in his garage-studio, hand painting beautiful logos and insignias. And there were always a nameless herd of transients roaming through the area, as my grandma's house was but a few blocks from the MKT tracks. It all made for a very interesting tableau.

I would come to learn many things about my grandma Nellie that week. I never saw her in anything but frumpy Calico dresses. She only "gussied up" once a month—when her social security check came and she walked down town to shop for groceries and pay bills. To the day she died, I never saw her in anything but those threadbare dresses. Her bread was always made from scratch—never purchased from the store. It was the most wonderful stuff I've ever eaten. For breakfast, she would meticulously slice it, butter the individual pieces and then fry them in a cast iron skillet over the stove. She then generously applied dollops of apple butter on her slices. Regular toast, you might imagine, was always sub-par after that.

She laboriously carried water in buckets from both Bill Brazier's backyard well and Pudd and Ode's. She loved Perry Como. She liked to sit on the front porch swing and sing "Old Shep," the shameless tear-jerker about a dog who grew up with a boy and saved his life when he was drowning. She also taught my older sister to sew on an old Singer treadle sewing machine.

She washed her hair in rainwater that collected in an old defunct washing machine that was located under a rain gutter on the back porch. For many years she used a chamber pot and outhouse until my Uncle Marlon built her a restroom complete with shower and toilet in 1964.

She taught Mickey how to sneeze on command. She warmed her bed in the winter by heating bricks on the wood stove and then placing them under the covers at the footboard. She never liked to travel too far from home and absolutely abhorred riding in a car—which explained, I thought, why she walked downtown once a month as opposed to riding with my Uncle Al. I rarely saw her smile—she had a sulphur-and-obsidian stare—and she seemed distrustful of everyone. On a good day she had the demeanor of an annoyed drill sergeant. While she seemed amenable to my being there that week, I always got the sense that she secretly thought I might be a communist spy. Or at the very least a Viet Nam war protester. Maybe even a federal employee.

One of the first realizations I came to there was the fact that time didn't just slow down in Erie, KS. It didn't even freeze. Like a glacier in reverse, it actually crept backward. From grandma's depression-era wardrobe to the pot-bellied wood-burning stove to Uncle Al's obsession with the 1950's, it was like seeing my school history books springing to life. And I don't mean that in a good way.

After that first day, we all settled into a gentle routine that would, for the most part, be part and parcel of my visit there. We would all begin the day at the kitchen table for one of grandma's signature breakfasts, then I would wait for approximately 4 hours while Uncle Al showered, dressed, smoked a pipe, preened and posed in front of the mirror, slicked and combed his hair, smoked a pipe, and posed some more until he decided that he looked as close to James Dean as he would ever get.

We had exactly four stops to make in one afternoon—Richie's Rexall Drugs, Kelly Drive-in and Country Kitchen Café—and finally to the junkyard just off of the new US59.

Of those languid June afternoons spent with my idiosyncratic uncle, I most enjoyed the trips to the eateries. There I could wolf down all of the Shasta Cream Soda and homemade banana cream pie I could tolerate without getting physically ill—and watch with scarcely concealed amusement as every single one of my uncle's advances were rebuffed with surgical precision by every waitress in every joint—even the one with hair on her upper lip and a tattoo of a howling wolf on her arm.

To get to those greasy spoons, though, meant making an assumption that my uncle's 1953 Ford would start and then stay running until we returned safely home that evening.

After sliding in the front seat that first trip, I was immediately horrified and titillated at the same time. Taped to the metal dashboard of uncle's car were various and sundry pictures of naked women—blondes, brunettes, redheads and some whose hair was of indeterminate color. And, in an effort, I suppose, to lessen the shock, there was also a calendar sponsored by the local COOP grain elevator attached to the driver's side sun visor.

The photographs were not the kind of wooden, android-like women I would see in the JC Penney or Wards catalog lingerie sections, nor the spear-carrying, loin-clothed jungle vixens found in an occasional *National Geographic* at the public library. No, these were young, pretty young women with absolutely no clothes on. Now I knew for sure that grandma never got in his car for a lift downtown.

Unfazed by my obvious speechless, awkward demeanor, Uncle Al fired up the beast, and with a puff of light blue smoke from the rusted tailpipe, we backed out of the driveway and headed down Massachusetts.

After the first four days of this uninterrupted routine, it suddenly dawned on me that while the rest of young America was enjoying the "Summer of Love," I on the other hand was experiencing the "Summer of Junk." This clearly called for a deviation. And it would involve faking an illness and trespassing on forbidden property.

There was an old dilapidated red barn in the rear of my grandma's yard that had in years past been the domain of farm animals. Now, due to Uncle Al's success at foraging garbage, it had become a repository for what I assumed were his most treasured artifacts. I was warned by both uncle and grandma not to even attempt to go in there—the place was full of poisonous snakes and spiders ready to paralyze and kill their next victim. Obviously, something very cool was in that barn. And I needed to find out what it was.

On the fifth day of my visit, I feigned a sore throat and even manufactured a few good coughs so as to bail out on my uncle. Then, as the afternoon sun sagged to the west, my grandma settled down to her daily afternoon nap. As she laid sawing logs in her bed, I tiptoed out the front door and headed down the 4 X 4 boards that served as a makeshift sidewalk to the barn. I fairly ran down the planks as thoughts of Copperheads and Rattlesnakes leaping up to bite me on the leg flooded my mind.

At once I was inside the forbidden, crumbling structure. To my surprise, it wasn't *full* of junk. It was only about half-full. Immediately, I began rummaging through all of it, trying to figure out what crown jewel they were trying to conceal with their scary-snakes exhortations. Soon, I found it. I am not sure that it was the reason that grandma didn't want anyone out there, but I was fairly confident that it was definitely the reason Uncle Al guarded the place like it was Ft. Knox.

I opened the flaps of a dust-covered box to at first see an old issue of *Famous Monsters of Filmland*, one of my favorite magazines. As the box appeared to be full of glossies, I thought I had hit the mother lode of monster mania. But when I moved the first mag, the one underneath was an oddly named publication called *Gent*. Deeper I dug. I came across one called *Lowdown*. Then *Girl Parade*. It was now obvious—I had discovered Uncle Al's hidden stash of booby books. It was the mother lode all right—of naked women.

There was no question—it was my duty to smuggle at least one back to Chanute to share with my buddies. This singular event would make me a virtual hero, as no one in our group had access to any—even if most of the women in the rags looked like Ernest Borgnine. Carefully, I removed the *Famous Monsters of Filmland* cover and inserted one of the treasured nudie books in it—a pristine copy of *Monsieur*. Later that day, I told Uncle Al and grandma that I found the monster mag in one of the many mountains in the yard—and could I have it?

Of course they said 'yes,' and I thought for just a split second that uncle was giving me a knowing look, but such was my mania to have a boobie magazine to share with my friends, that I confidently stashed it away in my suitcase. This was to be, unfortunately, the highlight of my trip to Erie that summer—other than hearing the gruesome news that Jayne Mansfield had been decapitated in a horrible car accident. "She was the blonde movie star with the big cans," Uncle Al dutifully informed me when I inquired as to who she was.

The thought of that big-titted body without a head would haunt me for the few remaining nights in Erie.

I was mostly at complete odds with my grandma and uncle. I preferred to listen to the Top 40 on WHB AM-71 Radio. They liked the twang of country crooner's such as Ernest Tubbs and Jim Reeves. How they watched vapid crap-trap like *Hee Haw* and *Glenn Campbell's Goodtime Hour* on their rabbit-eared, snowy television set confounded me. I wanted to catch my staples such as *Rowan & Martin's Laugh-In* and *The Smothers Brothers*. Usually I just waited for uncle to fall asleep in his easy chair in front of the TV and then watched what I wanted until the last of three stations signed off with the "High Flight" tribute.

Often, I too, would fall asleep, only to wake up to the dull drone of the Indian test pattern screen.

Then, after what seemed like decades, Sunday arrived, and with it Mrs. Jenkins. "No," I informed her after she asked me if any of the cafes in Erie served chili cones, "but I had a great time anyway." Of course it was a lie. The only redeeming thing about my visit there was located deep in my suitcase now lying in her trunk. And they all had heads, thank God.

On the way out of town, we passed the little house on the corner of South Lincoln and West 4th Street where mom, dad and us kids lived until divorce shattered the family. I had no real memories there, just shards of murky recollection. I could not even remember what dad's face looked like anymore. Seeing the old house as we sped by did nothing to help improve my recall.

The evening sky was the color of caramel as we lumbered onto US59 and on to Chanute via old Shaw Road. It hadn't rained all week, and the Neosho River and its tributaries were gingerly back in their banks. Little did I know that I would never again spend that kind of time at my grandma and Uncle Al's. My little sister and I visited for a couple of days there at Christmas break in December 1969. And for a few days in the Spring of 1970, grandma and uncle came to Chanute to help my mother take care of my new baby brother, Tim.

I can't recall seeing either of them again after that.

Grandma died in 1979. It was the only time I saw her out of her signature calico dresses—and with her hair down. She never got to see my first son born just one month later. Uncle Al died of a massive heart attack in March 1982. After ice and snow had prevented him from driving downtown to Richie's, he apparently had walked there and back. Upon reaching home, he succumbed, and they later found him face-down on his bed.

Eventually, the house and land were sold—and the new owners razed the structure and cleared the lot. Now there is a charming walkout rancher there, but it doesn't in any way resemble the old homestead. Because, I guess, of all the eccentricities surrounding my grandma and Uncle Al, all future dysfunctional family behaviors would come to be attributed to "The Erie Connection."

And rightfully so.

ROCKET MAN

IT WAS ASTONISHING TO ME how many things could change in just one week. By the time I got back from the Erie trip, mom had a job, a new boyfriend—Floyd Watkins—and a new friend, Johnny Paul, who looked like a holdover from the 50's with his black leather jacket and ducktail haircut. Both men were regulars at some of the local watering holes. Little sister had also made some new acquaintances down the block and Darren and Jerome were busy swimming and enjoying the summer movies at People's. The best thing about returning to my humdrum life in Chanute was the lifting of all sanctions that had been placed on me for the shoplifting incident.

That meant a resumption of watching *Wrestling With Russ Davis* on Saturday nights. *Wrestling With Russ Davis* was basically a bunch of pro wrestling matches from the 1950's filmed at the old Chicago Amphitheater and broadcast on our NBC affiliate, KOAM-TV. It was decadent fun to watch such sport stalwarts as Dick the Bruiser, Killer Kowalski, Hans Schmidt, Verne Gagne, Chief Don Eagle and nameless others ply their trade with such exotic and diabolical throws as The Sleeper Hold, The Piledriver, Full Nelson, Chokehold, etc. Of course, I tried them all out successfully on my hapless little sister, who was always the "bad" guy who never won a match.

Mom's new job was one that I was not particularly fond of, but one that in hindsight I should have predicted was in the cards. As she had already spent considerable time as a paying customer at the E & M Tavern, a dark and dingy mom-and-pop beer joint on East Main Street, it was, I guess, only following the natural order that she soon elevated herself to barkeep. Though the E & M was a straight-shot 3-block journey down the alley from our house, I never felt comfortable with the thought of her walking home alone at night after closing time. So on those warm summer nights when the skies filled with fireflies and after the last match on *Wrestling With Russ Davis*, I scampered down the darkened alley and through the back door of the bar to escort my mom safely home. Not that a twelve year old boy could do much to thwart an attack, mind you.

It was also a chance, however brief, to talk with her one on one about a whole variety of subjects.

During one of these walks, she suggested—advised might be the more accurate term—that I might want to attend an upcoming church camp with the family down the block that little sister had befriended— the Cooper's.

"Just go with them to church first to see if it is something that you might like to do," she reasoned. "Maybe you could even make some new friends."

Never mind that I already knew what I wanted to do—hang out with friends that I already had, ride bikes, eat chili cones and swim at the pool. The Coopers were a nice young couple with two rambunctious sons who attended the Assembly of the Highest God, a non-denominational church headed up by a fire-and-brimstone preacher. As a trial run, I accompanied them to services for a couple of Sundays before deciding that, yes, camp sounded like a fun idea—even if some of the people in the congregation spoke in tongues and writhed around on the floor during the sermon. "Have you been saved?" the pastor bellowed to me one Sunday from his pulpit high above the huddled masses. "Do you know Jesus?"

"I… I'm not sure," I stammered embarrassingly, not realizing that there was going to be a question-and-answer session. I was then promised that I would be 'baptized' during my one week stay at church camp. Having come from a family that *never* attended church and didn't know the difference between a Methodist and an Episcopalian, the word conjured up some strange images. Mr. Cooper reassured me that it was just a simple ceremony where I would be dunked in some water after a short prayer to invite Christ in my life. Given some of my more recent transgressions, this didn't sound like such a bad idea.

We left for camp at the beginning of the second week in July,

1967 in a rickety, retired school bus with oxidized yellow paint that I was sure was going to break down en route. The complex was located in rural Butler County, Kansas a few miles from the little town of Augusta, or roughly 90 miles from home. Shortly after arriving, I along with countless others, decided that we didn't want to be there after all and wanted to go home. We found out immediately that though homesickness was normal, no one got to go home early excepting illness or injury. It was crowded, cramped, disorganized and full of kids from all over the state of Kansas. There were no radios or televisions and it seemed like all we ever did was chores. And attend classes. Basically it was like having to go to school and work at a job—in the middle of summer when I should be having fun, no less.

My baptism took place near the end of the week in the Whitewater River, a meandering tributary that had a crooked bend at the south end of the camp. It was comedic irony that my ablution occurred in a Mississippi watershed river named Whitewater. The waters were unseasonably cold and the color of an old Army blanket. I went back to my room afterwards ebullient with the newfound power of Christ, but smelling of fish and leaving a trail of mud all of the way from the bus drop-off point to my bathroom.

The 90-mile trip back home was made at night and was all the more scary because of it. All I could think about on the journey was that summer was half over and I hadn't been swimming or to a movie once. Sitting in the seat next to me, Mr. Cooper offered rather casually that those activities were "sinful" and now that I was a child of the Lord, it would not be in my best interest to pursue them any longer. And, he intoned, to be more pure, I would need to cease the wearing of shorts in the summer. Long pants, he reasoned, were the proper attire for young men of my age.

I was confused. What did wearing shorts and attending movies have to do with religion? It was obvious that there was much for me to learn. I had no idea that Jesus preferred blue jeans.

My education regarding such manners came to a screeching halt one sultry Sunday morning in late July. I was not feeling well and had decided to stay home rather than attend services. Naturally, this did not sit well with Mr. Cooper, who engaged in a spirited debate with my mom through our front screen door. Though I was upstairs and in bed and could only hear fragments of their conversation, the gist of it was that if I didn't go to church, I would probably be banished to Hell. "He is sick, Mr. Cooper," my mom insisted.

Their interchange slowly escalated to a full-fledged argument which culminated in Mr. Cooper being asked to leave our porch and property. "You do not have to go to that church with those people any longer," mom would later say to me. Though she wasn't a religious person, she encouraged me to find my own way, my own journey of faith—and not be fooled by charlatans. "God doesn't care if you wear shorts or go to the public swimming pool," she assured me. "He cares if your heart is pure." No preacher would ever speak words that rang with such truth.

With the Erie and Assembly of the Highest God detours now behind me, the summer of 1967 began to take on a more orderly sameness. The daily walk to the public swimming pool was about 1 ½ miles and took me through downtown Chanute. Every Friday I stopped in a unique little music shop on Main Street called Evans Music to pick up WHB's 40 Star Super Hit Survey, a compendium of the week's top music. Evans was much more than a depository of top 40 music lists, however.

It seemed you could purchase just about anything musical there, from instruments such as drums, woodwinds, guitars and flutes to sheet music, long-playing records, 45 RPM's, spindle inserts and private lessons. None of which would have done me any good given that my only talent for music was merely a deep appreciation of it. Besides, I just wanted to see how far up the charts "Light My Fire" by the Doors had climbed.

It was about this time that I began to ponder the school year that lie only one month ahead. To be sure, it was a big step leaving behind the relative comfort of a neighborhood grade school for Royster Junior High School—where all of the combined elementary school prisoners converged into a 600-member army. And then there was the school mascot to contemplate—the Rockets. Not to be outdone, the high school mascot was the Blue Comets.

While I thought it was ultra-cool to live in a town where the team mascots were *not* the everyday garden variety of Lions, Hawks and Bulldogs, I couldn't help but wonder how the space-themed representative symbols of our junior and high school came to be, when and by whom. There would be time enough, I reasoned, in the future to solve such delicate mysteries.

Darren and I had gotten back into a groove of movie-going and pinball machine-playing that required a steady stream of revenue that we, unfortunately, did not have. We were no longer helping Jerome with the paper route, so in the absence of earned income, we turned to the only other possible source of cash—Darren's Uncle Ned. Ned Kelly had a predictable routine of working all night in his brother's bakery shop—swilling his favorite beverage all the while—and then passing out in the early morning hours on the sofa in the living room of Darren's house, where he was allowed to stay. This allowed Darren the chance to rifle through the old man's pants pockets for loose bills and change, which he did so with the absolute and uncanny expertise of an Italian pickpocket fleecing an unsuspecting tourist in Rome. He was agile, adroit, well-practiced and fleet of foot—all of the virtues needed for the funding of an afternoon of movies, chili cones, pinball games and soda pop.

Naturally we felt guilty, so when the opportunity arose to work with Uncle Ned in the bakery for a few weeks, we pounced on it. Not only did it give us the chance to *earn* spending money, we also got to stay up all night—something every normal, red-blooded 12 year old American kid pined for.

The walk to the bakery, which was but three blocks away, began around 1:00AM in the morning. The sensation of being able to trek down the middle of Grant Street, normally a heavily-trafficked thoroughfare during the daylight hours, was a fanciful paradox. There was a quiet swish of trees laden with leaves that screened out the moon and splashed odd shadows on the cooling bricks of the street. A dog barked faintly in the background. It was as if we were the only human beings alive and awake.

Once the lights were clicked on at the shop, though, the whimsical dream came to an abrupt halt. I never realized how much hard work went into making glazed doughnuts and long johns. Materials had to be off-loaded from supply trucks and stacked on pallets in the basement. Then those same sacks of flour, wheat, sugar, yeast and other ingredients were transferred to containers for use in the baking process. Racks had to be cleaned, mixers and dividers washed and dried, and fryers cooled and scrubbed. There was barely enough time to sample the wonderful, unforgettable and aromatic sweet delights that Mr. Kelly and Uncle Ned inevitably created.

The walk back home at around 9:00AM was quite different in the warming glare of day, the traffic on Grant Street relegating our journey to the sidewalks. It was an odd and extraordinary two weeks of working all night and sleeping all day. The funny thing was that I never once missed swimming at the pool, going to the movies or any of the other activities that we normally partook of during daylight hours. The departure from the accustomed was so profound and such a welcome relief that we barely noticed the beginning of the new school year was barely two weeks away.

By the time Labor Day Weekend had arrived, mom had resigned her position as chief bar-maid at the E&M Tavern, scrapped her relationship with Floyd Watkins and outfitted me with all of the accoutrements I would need for life at Royster Junior High School. Only then did I finally and harshly arrive at the conclusion that the next three years were going to be radically different than the previous nine. I was going to have to *shower* with other boys. This thought naturally filled me with dread and horror.

My school schedule also required that I take woodshop. I knew nothing of power saws, lathes, sanders and rotary tools, so this was also a terrifying notion in which I could imagine myself losing fingers in a planer accident or being hit with a two by four sent flying by a faulty table saw. Ultimately, I couldn't determine which scenario would be worse—parading around naked with a bunch of boys or grappling with a runaway joiner.

Perhaps the only inviting thing about entry into 7th grade was the fact that the school itself was new. In fact, as we were about to find out, it was so new that it was not altogether completed. Gone was the old red-brick building with the concrete keystones that closely resembled the high school. The new structure consisted of blonde brick reminiscent of 1950s ranch style homes, but was modern by the standards of the day. The only building remaining from the original complex was the Trade School. It sat on the northeast corner of the compound and was connected to the cafeteria and main building by wooden planks that were discarded during construction.

Three of my six classes that first year were to be held there. In a tragic lottery of logistics, my first semester schedule revealed one major flaw—classes in the Trade School and main building were in between each other, meaning that I would spend one hour in the old building and then have to walk the planks of death to the new building for one hour and then repeat the process two more times. To and from the old and new, all day…

When school actually commenced after Labor Day, the back-and-forth scenario was revealed to contain yet another fatal Catch-22. As landscaping was one of those punch-list items that appeared to have been overlooked, the ground between the Trade School and the other buildings was a curious mixture of dirt, nails, mortar and brick remnants that quickly turned into the La Brea Tar Pits with the commencement of autumn rains. One slip off of the heavily-traveled planks and an unsuspecting student could end up in the muck, where anthropologists in the future would find their bones perfectly preserved. In retrospect it sort of took the edge off the jitters about showering with other boys and being mortally wounded in shop class.

That first year as Rocket Man was most difficult for me. I did not have Charles or Darren in any of my classes. My math teacher did not have the patience for my lack of talent with numbers and had probably decided in those first few weeks that I was going to be given a D just so she wouldn't have to deal with me as a repeat customer. My shop teacher was—no surprise here—missing several digits and expected all of us to manufacture a complete bedroom ensemble in our first semester. My first completed piece was a small lamp that looked like the Brooklyn Bridge. Literally.

My gym teacher was 94 years old but could climb the 20' rope all of the way to the top and down again *without* using his legs. Early in the year we had to, as one of our learning experiences in physical education, don boxing gloves and square off against random competition. I drew the only black kid in the class—and he weighed about 210 pounds and had dizzyingly fast hands—so naturally I went down to a spectacular and inglorious defeat. And in record time, I might add.

While I cherished art class, our teacher was so Laissez-faire that the most fun in her course was determining how long certain insects could last in the pottery kiln and launching 10' paper airplanes out the second story window toward the marching band that practiced on the adjoining softball fields. I wanted to draw or paint pictures—not make cheap, junk jewelry for my mom, who I reasoned would promptly lose, break or throw it away anyway.

Science class was no better. Being of the creative mind, I was by contrast a veritable village idiot when it came to how stuff works and predictable outcomes. The instructor was also the vice principal and seemed to single me out for specialized persecution. When it came time to perform the requisite dissection of a formaldehyde-soaked frog, I took a cue from Muhammad Ali's refusal to be inducted into the U.S. military by saying "I ain't got no quarrel with them frogs." He was not amused. I began to miss many of his classes due to "illness."

Just when I couldn't imagine things getting any worse, they did in the form of a pink slip from the office interrupting another mind-numbing 60 minutes of fraction decimal conversion in math. Normally I would have derived great pleasure to get out of her class, but when the pink slip directed me to report to the guidance counselor's office, I became a little concerned. As it turned out, it was well-warranted concern.

Apparently, on the Saturday evening prior, someone had broken out many of the windows on the north side of the high school. An eyewitness had already come forward with claims that I was the person responsible. I was asked in quick succession my whereabouts, would I take a lie detector test and was I aware of the punishment for such a crime.

Of course, I did not commit the crime that I was being blamed for, but I was floundering in front of the guidance counselor out of cold, abject fear. I knew how serious the crime was and what the possible consequences were. I felt it was terribly wrong to have someone blame me yet I was not made aware of my accuser. I offered to take the polygraph test and meet with police. Satisfied, I was released from the counselor's office. Never before or since was I so happy to be back in math class.

Apparently my eager willingness to be tested and meet with officials soon discounted me as a viable suspect. Schoolyard grapevines and rumor mills finally revealed my accuser about the same time that he recanted his eyewitness testimony. I was finally cleared of the crime I never committed.

This seemingly small and inconsequential episode in my young life had a very disquieting and long-lasting effect on me afterward, though. I began to not trust my fellow man quite so much and resented that I was already ostracized and in the process of being branded a "troublemaker" by fellow students, teachers and law enforcement personnel.

Now I knew how Fatty Arbuckle, a silent film comedian who survived a Hollywood scandal in the 1920s, must have felt. Sometimes, even after vindication, the hurt lingers and can erode confidence in the system and one's self. There were many dark days after the incident in which I questioned my life and the direction I was taking it. Why did my dad desert me? Were my friends enriching my life or tearing it down? Was I a classic under-achiever or did I just suck at math, science and wood shop?

Like the exchange between Alice and The Cat in *Alice In Wonderland*, I figured that my destination didn't matter as long as I didn't care how I got there. I was at a fork in the road—proverbially speaking. Things needed to change.

I was delivered from the abyss of depression by my second semester English teacher, a kindly oval woman who must have seen some glimmer of talent in my written musings. Encouraged by her to submit one of my essays for the end-of-the-school year writing contests, I did so and won first prize for 7th graders.

I was never so proud as I was that clear, warm May day that was so pretty that janitors left the doors to the gymnasium open. In front of 600 cheering students I accepted the award, celebrated after school with Darren and Jerome wolfing down chili cones at Barker's Dairy Bar and then went home to an empty house.

Eighth grade would surely be better.

RITES OF PASSAGE

THE END OF MY SEVENTH grade school year couldn't have come quick enough. At the onset of 1968, world and local events began to spin out of control and sometimes challenged each other for importance. I am sure, for instance, that few fellow classmates attached much importance to the fact that the forces from the Viet Cong and North Vietnamese armies had launched a highly coordinated military campaign against the South and U.S. troops in January of that year. It came to be called the Tet Offensive and some strategists would later say that the war turned on this singular event.

Even fewer were aware, two months later, of the atrocities of My Lai, where the mass murder of hundreds of unarmed citizens in South Vietnam by U.S. Army soldiers took place the day after my 13th birthday. Details of the massacre would not fully come to light for more than a year, however. These were unsettling global occurrences for a kid just trying to remember his locker combinations and to bring his gym clothes home once a week to be laundered.

In April we moved from the large, two-story roach-infested house on Walnut Street to a small clapboard bungalow on South Grant right across the street from Santa Fe's large classification yard. This latest relocation was not as disruptive as previous ones, though, in that it did not require us to change schools. That I was getting somewhat numb to the fact that we seemed to move every couple of years also helped.

It took a while, though I must now admit, to get used to the banging of rail cars as their switchers pushed them across the yard and into rows of other boxcars. As most of the switching seemed to occur at night, I soon learned how to relegate the horrific explosions into a form of white noise—at least to the point where I could get a good night's sleep.

It was always highly entertaining, however, to observe an overnight guest bolt upright and out of bed in abject terror at the sound of the first catastrophic coupling. "Rookie," I would mumble and then drift back to sleep.

On April 4th of that year, Martin Luther King was gunned down in Memphis, Tennessee at the young age of 39. Riots broke out in hundreds of cities across the country soon after, including Kansas City, 120 miles to the north. Rumors that bands of looting and pillaging protesters from that area were heading for our fair city made their way through the stunned populace. We were filled with dread and sure that our little town would be torched and burned to the ground. Mom's reassurance that everything would be alright came in the form of her announcement that she was pregnant.

It worked. After that shocker I instantaneously forgot about having to defend the town from big-city thugs. "His name is Bill and you will get to meet him soon," she promised, describing the father. We will be getting married in a few months, also." Mom was better than the KBI at protecting clandestine information. Hell, I didn't even know she had a boyfriend.

My friendships with Darren, Jerome and Charles had begun to change as the school year trudged on. I spent less time with them and instead started to percolate new relationships with a variety of classmates. It was only a matter of time before I hitched my wagon to two of them—Jason Black and Donnie Hildebrandt.

Jason had come to Chanute a year earlier by way of Kansas City. His dad divorced and became a truck driver for Manley Transfer, a local trucking outfit. Jason supposedly had an older brother. I never met him. There was a peculiar crescent-shaped scar on his left biceps which he attributed to a "little knife fight back home." He had cornflower silk blonde hair and baby blue eyes that belied his fierce nature.

Donnie was a freckle-faced gangly bundle of nervous energy. Like me, he performed marginally in school and seemed lost most of the time. He could be forgiven for that, however, as he lived in a household that was a real-life *Brady Bunch* episode. His dad, a tall, erudite window salesman with three other boys in tow besides Donnie, met and married

Sally, a fiery redhead homemaker with four girls, and they lived in a sprawling, dilapidated old Victorian on Highland Street. The place was a constant, disheveled beehive of activity and the noise levels were alarmingly high. In short, their lives were nothing like the *Brady Bunch*.

As one might expect, my mother warned me repeatedly about my burgeoning alliance with Jason and Donnie. "They're bad kids going nowhere," she intoned. They are no better than the three hooligans you run with now," she added. I wasn't about to be mollycoddled, though, and pretty much disregarded her advice as being over-protective and reactionary.

Donnie's house was only about a mile from ours, but the quickest route took Jason and I through Santa Fe's sprawling railroad yards where faded yellow and blue diesels plied their service on at least 25 sets of tracks. Naturally, the brakemen and switchmen did not care for a couple of ne'er do well teenagers dodging and climbing over and under trains in the complex. We soon developed a method of crossing that involved some very stealthy characteristics.

Together, the three of us embarked on a series of challenges, or dares if you will, that made climbing the water tower and flipping people the bird on Main Street look like child's play. Eventually, we would become obsessed with seeing how close we could walk to the edge of the cliff without teetering over. If this was nowhere, as mom warned, I definitely wanted to go there.

Based on our observations in the flat-shunt classification yard, the first dare that we undertook was boxcar running. This involved identifying a long string of unmoving boxcars and then gathering at one end. Once there, we climbed up the access ladder to the catwalk. Then we proceeded to run down the entire length of cars—one after the other—until we reached the far end.

Now this might not seem to be a dangerous, life-threatening caper until you consider that our 'runs' were always conducted at night and there was always the omnipresent danger of an engine coupling onto the boxcars, tripping off the catwalks or falling into gondolas or onto flatbeds that were sometimes placed in the middle of a series of same-size boxcars. Not to mention that boxcar running was illegal. It was exhilarating and pulse-quickening, though, and the benefits seemed, at least on the surface, to outweigh the dangers. This would be an activity that we indulged in often throughout the Summer of 1968.

Barely two weeks out of school, Bobby Kennedy's assassination by Sirhan Bishara Sirhan in Los Angeles on June 5th seemed to take the collective winds out of the nation's sails. His death the very next day was devastating. What once looked like a smooth run to the party nomination and eventual presidency was now a black crepe funeral train to Arlington National Cemetery. It was almost too much for many Americans. They lined up in cities, towns and farms all along the route, many crying and asking 'why?' Even I, a 13-year old kid living in a small Midwestern town, wondered what had gone wrong with our once-proud nation. "Where will it all end?" I asked to no one in particular. It was just as well, however, as there was no one there to answer.

As with all global, national and local crises, though, life soon began to resume its customary ebb and flow.

Our next adventure took place on the Neosho River northeast of the city. By June of 1968 the river was running slightly over normal flood stage and was teeming with channel catfish and flatheads. On several occasions we hiked out past fields of chest-high corn to Brown Wells Dam, a concrete levee constructed by the Army Corp of Engineers to combat overflowing after the great Flood of '51. There, oblivious to the hands of the clock, we pitched our tent, fished from a small sandbar just downstream from the dam and swam in the murky waters.

It was during one of these summer campouts that we discovered a long, thick cable stretching approximately one hundred feet across the river. It was at least thirty feet in the air and anchored on each bank by large concrete pilings. The cable was thick, twisted and braided and held aloft suspension style by little u-type baskets every twenty feet or so.

I am unsure who actually originated the idea, but soon enough all three of us had scaled the piling on the east bank (where our campsite was) and were hanging on the cable and going across above the river hand-over-hand. I think it was about midway, dangling thirty feet above the swift, brown current that I realized that I was tired and wanted to go back. The problem was that in turning around to go in the opposite direction required letting go with one hand. That would have left me briefly hanging from the cable with one hand—and I wasn't sure if my arm strength could hold up.

Given that, I followed Jason and Donnie hand-over-hand, inch by inch, all of the way across to the east bank and down the piling to the ground. I can't recall how long all of this took, but it seemed an eternity. All of us were winded, tired and sore. "Surely there is a spot in the river where we can swim back across." Donnie said. "I don't think any of us can make it back over the cable."

We all concurred that finding a shallow ford or less turbulent spot in the river was in our best interests. The problem was, despite wandering up and down the east bank for over an hour, we couldn't find one. Nor was there an access road. The closest bridge was seven miles downstream.

The only way back across the river to our campsite was the way we had come in the first place.

And so it was that we summoned the all of the strength remaining to climb the piling once again and undertake the arduous journey thirty feet in the air over a very swift, unforgiving current as the sun set behind the horizon. The sky became light purple, then eggplant and finally black. Fireflies sparkled around us. The wind from a warm front picked up from the south and began to rock us gently as we made our way to the other side.

I can't properly describe, even to this day, the intense fear I felt hanging by my two hands and moving slowly across the cable toward the safety of the west piling. As the stars came out one by one, I could no longer *see* the river, but I could still *hear* it churning below me. My heart was racing and I was so tired I ached—but I knew that I had to get all of the way across. There was no alternative.

We did make it across, of course, but that was one challenge that we did not care to repeat. None of us, not even Jason, the most battle-hardened of the group, was interested in testing the cable and the river again. We pan-fried our channel catfish that night, drank the last of our Shasta sodas and slept the sleep of kings beside a crackling fire. We awoke to a morning thunderstorm and hiked back to town in a driving rain.

Just north of Chanute, and slightly west of Highway U.S. 169, the Katy railroad snaked through dense woods and across Village Creek, a tributary of the Neosho, on a timber trestle. That was another of our favorite fishing holes. There in the brackish, slow-moving waters, we caught innumerable bullhead with chicken livers and live bait. Box turtles sunned themselves on logs. Occasionally, an oxidized red Katy engine hauling a couple of gondolas full of aggregates would trundle over the old bridge, lending the air creaking and groaning noises.

Nearby, there was a curious escarpment with a small cave and what looked like a chimney cut into it. This geological anomaly was called Indian Cave, and was well-known to most locals. The chimney was probably cut sometime after Cherokee Indian tribes had relinquished the area to settlers. During prohibition, it was rumored that the location was used as an outdoor beer garden or gin mill. On a gentle ridge overlooking the cave and bridge there was a large, tumble-down hay barn.

If the fish weren't biting, we would often put down our Zebcos and pick up our BB Guns—which we took with us on seemingly every outdoor adventure. And as the reader might have guessed, we eventually turned them on each other. Between the wonderful old cave, the woods thick with Cottonwoods and Elms, the hay barn with its loft high above the landscape, the area was a natural for BB Gun wars. To top it all off, there was, at the location where the railroad tracks crossed the highway, an abandoned, crumbling brick building full of odd and fantastic machinery.

Rumors were that this old building was once a slaughterhouse—where animals of some sort were killed and processed into meat foods. Whatever it had been in its previous lifetime, we soon converted the decaying structure into another BB Gun war settlement. It was a great place to hide or snipe the enemy from and was full of neglected conveyor belts, holding pens, hangers as well as tables and lockers.

I had come a long way from the days of shooting at my friends with toy rifles at Elmwood Cemetery. To go home from the Indian Cave Shootouts was to do so with a variety of injuries. Depending on the distance and trajectory the BB traveled, damage to the victim could be shockingly disparate—an ugly welt on an arm, a reddish indention on the soft tissue of the back, an actual BB embedded under a bloody lump on the leg, etc. Naturally, we always kept our injuries secret from our parents—even if it meant throwing away a bloodstained shirt in Village Creek.

As it always did, the seasonal clock ticked away in the dog days of summer, 1968. We still explored the drainage canal and climbed the old water tower, but soon the Goldenrods were in full bloom along the railroad tracks leading into the woods at Indian Cave—a sure sign that summer, at least in the sense that we knew it, was about to expire. In Chicago, in the waning days of August, the Democratic party elected Hubert Humphrey to be its nominee for President of the United States. This was amidst a backdrop of protest and violence by such groups as the Yippies, Students For A Democratic Society and the National Mobilization Committee to End the War—among others.

The year had been full of rage and showed no signs of abating.

Soon, 8th grade began at Royster Junior High and with it a new schedule to memorize, locker combinations to remember and a fresh group of 7th grade girls to ogle and objectify. The first real chance to disprove that my friends and I were hopeless social rejects with no chance to interact with real live females came during the Fall Festival street dance on an unusually cold late September night. Following the traditional parade that day, and after the Main Street merchants had closed their doors for business, hay bales were brought in for the crowds and a flat bed trailer for the musicians.

There were plenty of girls to meet and even dance with that night— had any of us known how to two-step or move to a fiddle or steel guitar. Instead, Jason, Donnie and I decided to embark on another adventure more suited to night and a definite chill in the air.

The old Johnson Hospital sat dark and discarded at the corner of 1st and Evergreen Streets, just a block from the lively and loud street dance. The deserted building was the antithesis of the gaiety taking place on Main Street—foreboding with an undercurrent of danger. Johnson Hospital had, until 1959 when Neosho Memorial Hospital opened on the west side of town, served Chanute's residents with diagnoses, treatments, x-rays, etc. After its service to residents as a medical facility, the building began a slow slide downhill as a clinic, a nursing home and finally flop house to transients and squatters.

With no electrical service, the three-story gray stucco and concrete edifice beckoned at night with windows that appeared as empty eye sockets. The front door was always ajar, an open mouth inviting the curious and fatally inquisitive.

Naturally, we decided to see just exactly went on in this old building. And what better time than a starless, cold and blustery late

September night with leaves blowing about and the strum and twang of homegrown country music permeating the smoky air?

The idea was for us to make our way into the building and up to the farthest third floor room and then back down again—without being accosted by any of the vagrants that happened to be in the place. It sounds relatively easy until you remember that there was no electrical power to the building and none of us had in our possession a flashlight. There would be no elevator service to the top floor and down again.

It took a few moments for my eyes to acclimate to the total and complete darkness of the entry and hallway of the ground floor. Once they did a faint glow from the Main Street activities filtered through the dirty windows and between the broken blind slats. The effect was eerie and disconcerting.

As the three of us made our way down the hallway toward the stairs leading up, we became aware of stirrings from within some of the rooms—shadowy movements and whispered cries and moans—an awakening of the dead. Foul odors wafted in and out of my nose— alcohol, feces, urine, and mold. It was a heavy bouquet of abominable smells.

The second floor was more of the same, only now it seemed some of the zombie-like figures had arose to check out the new interlopers. My pulse was racing. We practically flew down the hall to the staircase leading to the third and final floor. Ambient light found that top floor more easily and we could see mattresses scattered about on the floors along with broken glass and discarded food containers and cigarette butts. The individual rooms had been stripped of anything possibly and remotely valuable.

A couple of the transients had made it up the staircase to the third floor and were nearly at the top when we collectively decided to head back down. Despite not knowing the logistical layout of the building, we gambled and ran down the hallway to the opposite end of the wing. There, an identical staircase led down to the second, and presumably the first floor as well. Luckily, thankfully, we encountered no transients as we descended the east stairwell and onto the ground floor.

We could hear them shuffling not far behind us, though, calling to us with strange, unintelligible sounds. Bounding out the front door and down the steps, Jason, Donnie and I all felt incredibly relieved—and unbelievably exhilarated. We didn't stop running until we reached the relative safety of Main Street and the dancing country minions. There, under strands of bright fresco lights we sat on a hay bale and recounted the experience, laughing at the sheer lunacy of it. No wonder none of the girls wanted to dance or have anything to do with us.

We really were crazy.

We couldn't have known then, but this would be the last of the Fall Festival celebrations in Chanute.

In October mom got married for the third time to the father of her unborn baby, a short and stocky man named Bill. She told us he drove a truck that moved mobile homes, but we were also informed at various times that he was a pilot, an FBI agent and a military operative among other less glamorous professions. If he ever lived in our little white house on Grant Street, I don't recall it. He just kind of came and went on his own schedule.

The 1968 Olympics were held in October in Mexico City that year and featured more of the absurdity that had plagued the year to date. On the 16th of October, two black athletes from the United States—Tommy Smith and John Carlos—gold and bronze medalists in the men's 200 meter event, stood on the award podium barefoot and raised black-gloved fists during the playing of the Star Spangled Banner. Depending on your view at the time, they were considered either traitorous lepers or heroes of unquestioned bravery.

As if to counterbalance Smith and Carlos—though he would always deny they had any part in his actions—George Foreman, our country's Heavyweight Boxing representative at the Olympics that year, knocked out the Soviet Union's veteran Jonas Cepulis and then proceeded to walk around the ring and bow to the audience all the while holding aloft an American flag.

On the home front, Halloween, with its phantasmagorical trappings, was fast approaching and for the first time in my life I wouldn't be worrying about what costume to wear. It was collectively decided that the three of us were too old to be trick-or-treating anymore. That was a childish activity more suited for Donnie's younger siblings and my little sister—not for us guys slowly growing into manhood. No, we decided on a much more interesting evening to celebrate All Hallow's Eve. But to pull it off, we would need someone with a car.

That came in the form of a friend of Donnie's older brother Andy. Melvin Parker was, like us, a social misfit who didn't fit in with the crowd. He was three years older than us, chain-smoked non-filter Winston's and owned a rusting 1958 Ford Fairlane 500 Club Victoria hardtop coupe that had once been metallic green. He was in love with Wilma Flintstone and predicted that he would be in Industrial Boys School by his junior year in high school. "Can I have your car while you are locked up?" I remember asking him during one particular imbecilic encounter. "No, idiot," he replied. "I plan to drive it off the cliff at Buffalo Quarry before I go. If you can dredge it up from the bottom, then I guess you can have it." I immediately started hatching a plan involving a crane and underwater divers…

But first things first.

We recruited Melvin to haul us out on Halloween night, which unfortunately fell on a Thursday that year, to a place few dared to go even in the daytime—Greenwood Cemetery. If ever there was a post card for haunted graveyards, an icon for shadowy figures lurking in the mist, a symbol of things that go bump in the night, Greenwood was it. For years, rumors had abounded about the dead rising from their graves, 'floating' blue lights and a crazy old woman caretaker who often chased curiosity seekers away from the place with a loaded shotgun. The cemetery was full of civil war dead and contained many unmarked graves that consisted only of a pile of stones.

It also had a prototypical cast iron entry gate with "Greenwood Cemetery" welded across the arch. To get there, Melvin had to haul us about 5 miles east of the city on K-39, turn right on a gravel road and then drive another couple of miles or so. With a lit cigarette dangling from his mouth glowing orange in the dark, he turned to Donnie and I in the backseat. "I'm just going to go through the gates to the far end of the cemetery and drop you sissies off. But I'm not sticking around. I'll park the car up the road about a half mile and wait. You have 15 minutes. If you are not back in that amount of time, you will be walking home. I'm not goofing around, ladies."

Only he didn't say 'goofing.'

The idea, similar in theory to the Johnson Hospital caper, was to get to the farthest point in the old cemetery—in this case the circular drive to the west—and then make our way back to Melvin's car. No mean feat, as this would entail running past the yawning graves, the floating blue lights and finally past the crazy, skeletal, white-haired, gun-wielding woman's shanty near the entrance—then on another half mile to the car.

It was 8:30 PM when we tooled through the entrance to Greenwood and down the narrow lane to the far west end of the cemetery. Melvin cut the lights to try and avoid being seen, but it only added to the eerie, spectral atmosphere. Once at the turnaround, he opened the door without leaving his seat and ordered everybody out. One by one we exited the idling Ford and stood stock still in the middle of the road.

Melvin sped out of the graveyard and was gone. I remember thinking how quiet it was. There wasn't even a breeze to stir the trees. Until, that is, until a sharp trilling from a nearby Screech Owl shattered the silence. Then, as if to embellish the bird call, off in the far distance, a rapid succession of yips from what sounded like several coyotes pierced the air. "Did you see that?" Donnie asked, pointing in the direction of the woods that flanked the road to the west.

"See what, you pussy?" Jason laughed.

"I think it was one of those shadow people," Donnie replied nervously. At about the same time as his sentence trailed off, the snapping of a nearby tree branch and the distinct resonance of footfalls on dead leaves sounded an alarm bell. At the opposite end of the cemetery a light suddenly blinked on the porch to the caretaker's shack. Wordless, we bolted as one and followed the shortest route from where we were to the old road that led to Melvin's car.

That meant stumbling across graves, knocking over urns and flower arrangements and leaping over old headstones. I was the fastest of the three and led the way. Peripherally, I saw the crazy old woman come out of the house, but all she had was a flashlight. She didn't need a shotgun—I got a good look at her face as she tried to cut us off at the front gate. Her skin was almost translucent and her hair a shocking snow white. She had no teeth and her hands were gnarled and like those of some malevolent skeleton. Cackling and waving her flashlight menacingly at us, we bounded out of her reach and out of the cemetery and were gone down the road to Melvin's car.

Arthur Brown's "Fire" was howling from WHB on his car radio. "How was it, girls?" he asked with more than a hint of sarcasm in his voice.

"You don't wanna know," Jason panted. "Just drive."

It was about 9:15 that night when the Ford rolled into town past the Neosho River bridge and over the K-39 overpass. Most of the trick-or-treaters had completed their rounds and were now either home or on their way there. We scuttled a plan to relieve a few of them of their goodies. The moon slid from behind clouds that had made the night so dark just a couple of hours earlier. I was the last to be dropped off by Melvin.

"Really," he smirked as ashes dropped from his Winston onto the floorboard, "How was it? Did you see anything?"

"You don't wanna know," I echoed Jason's words. As Melvin drove off cackling, the old car leaving strands of blue smoke trailing, I marched up the sidewalk wishing we had gone trick-or-treating. "Nevermore," I thought, laughing at last at the Poe-etic irony.

Nixon got elected a few days later and the grass on Suicide Hill was finally declared ready to go for all box sledders. We passed the weekends there until a few days before Thanksgiving. Then Jason came up with a novel idea—dropping a dummy off of the Lincoln Street Overpass. We made a trial run—sans the dummy—the day after Turkey Day, riding our bikes up to the highest point of the overpass. Leaning over the railing, all of us concurred that the joke probably looked better from the ground.

The stunt appeared to be underwhelming as the dummy would fall on seldom-used railroad tracks barely 25 feet down. We were certain that no one would see it, therefore defeating the entire purpose of the prank. What we longed for, what we expected was for any number of people to see the dummy fall from *somewhere* and call the police. By which time, we would be long gone. All of us could then laugh hysterically the next day when the news of the prank hit the *Chanute Tribune*.

The Tioga Hotel was an ideal candidate, being six stories and in the heart of downtown, but we knew that we could never get on the roof and past feisty Mr. Jenkins. The grain elevators behind the Manhattan Hotel were almost perfect, too, but we were painfully unaware of how to climb them.

The answer came as if delivered on a bolt of lightning. While scanning the landscape by the elevators, I noticed the north yard light tower of the Santa Fe Railroad jutting 80' into the air, making it Chanute's highest structure. A small ladder was accessible and went all of the way to a tiny crow's nest where workers could replace failed lamps. If we all agreed, it would be the most dangerous adventure we had yet undertaken. We all agreed.

By Saturday we were at Donnie's house, hiding in the third story parlor and stuffing some of his dad's old jeans and a flannel shirt with rolled up newspapers and anything with any weight that was deemed expendable. We worked on the dummy, which we named Drooper after one of the hosts of the *Banana Splits Adventure Hour* cartoon, from dawn until dusk, perfecting every feature. Launch time was set for Sunday, November 24th.

The morning dawned windy, cloudy and cold—a quintessential November day. I opened the garage door so that we could all park our bikes in a safe place and away from the watchful eye of authorities. We hid the dummy under an old Army blanket that I dug out of the clothes closet and trudged up the street for the two-block journey to the yard light tower. I'm sure that it didn't look suspicious to anyone in the neighborhood.

Once at the base of the tower, we uncovered our prized mannequin and handed him off to Jason, physically the strongest of the three, for the long trek up to the service platform. It was a good thing that we had all packed gloves as the rungs of the ladder were bone-chilling cold. Per our plan, Jason went up first followed by Donnie. I pulled up third. That arrangement allowed the dummy to be passed down if the lead man were to tire.

We never had to amend the plan, though, as Jason got Drooper all of the way to the top by himself. And it took less time than we had originally calculated. Once at the crow's nest, however, we discovered that the area was barely big enough for all three of us. And as the bank of lights was located on the south side of the platform, our only option was to throw Drooper from the north side—against a now howling wind.

It was at that time, as we sat uncomfortably 80' in the air quietly contemplating the small snag in our plans, that we could all feel the crow's nest swaying ever so gently back and forth. Had I known anything about structural engineering then I would have been comforted by the realization that the benevolent rocking was *normal*. Instead, we did what all thirteen year olds would do in that situation—panic. "Let's get out of here!" Donnie screamed.

With that, Jason hurled Drooper over the railing. We watched only momentarily as the dummy floated out away from the tower than came smashing back into it on a northerly gust. He then fell rather ungracefully the remaining 60', arms and legs flailing in abnormal positions and looking very much like a real human body. Even his eventual crash landing onto the frozen ground had a life-like look to it.

Deeming the caper an unqualified success, we fairly flew down the ladder. We weren't fast enough, though, to escape a railroad security agent who careened into the yard in an unmarked vehicle looking as if we had just interrupted his Sunday brunch. Come to find out, we had. "What in the hell do you boys think you're doing?" he asked dourly. Casting a furrowed glance at the crumpled dummy laying on the ground a few feet away, he asked, "Do you think this is funny?" Of course we did. Hell, we thought it was hilarious.

"No, sir," I offered apologetically. "If you will let us go, we promise to never do it again. Ever." The agent turned his back on us and gazed out over the unusually quiet classification yard as if he were temporarily distracted by some faraway sight or sound.

"I will let all of you go under one condition," he said, turning back, a small smile appearing on his otherwise stern face. "You boys stop the damn boxcar running, too."

"Deal," I replied without consulting the other two who were now looking at me with obvious contempt.

"Sellout," Jason muttered in my direction under his breath as the agent got in his car to return to his warm meal. "Pussy," Donnie added, "I can speak for myself."

I picked up the army blanket and the pieces of the dummy and ran to catch up with my two best friends who were already past the freight docks. "Guys," I implored, "I never meant any of it. I just didn't want to see us fined or locked up in jail."

They seemed placated by that, and we made small-talk, even laughing at the thought of Drooper smashing to earth. Picking up their bicycles from my garage Jason and Donnie disappeared down the brick street, going different directions at 2nd. Sleet had begun to fall. Sundays at our house were normally quiet and uneventful, so after the excitement at the rail yard, it was a welcome relief to turn on the TV and plop down on the couch. Sleep came easily.

Looking back, it was no wonder we indulged in such crazy dares and schemes. Surrounded by an endless aura of bad news, political assassinations, and a foreign war seemingly growing worse by the day, these adolescent adventures were a kind of counter-balance. They took our attention away from the grim realities of the day, however brief. They also built a comradeship between us that the rest of the world could not touch.

It didn't matter if we couldn't control world events or if the girls at school didn't like us—or even if I had a dad and step-dad that I never saw—and a new sibling on the way.

We had each other.

At least for now.

WINDS OF CHANGE

IN THE EIGHT YEARS SINCE my father had unceremoniously left our family, mom found work at a number of menial jobs—seamstress in a garment factory, bar maid, electronics assembler, among others. In between those times, we were on relief and survived only with the help of Uncle Sam, free or reduced school lunches and food stamps. Eking out a meager living and defying all odds seemed suited to mom—in fact she was cleverly deft at it. No one could stretch a dollar further or make a pot of goulash last longer.

In the Spring of 1968 she proudly announced the acquisition of a new job. She would be working for Day & Zimmerman, a "defense contractor." I naturally recognized that any gig with a DOD contractor would probably pay decent money and provide excellent bennies. The location was Parsons, Kansas, 37 miles to the southwest. This would mean carpooling, of course.

So far, so good.

Then, after a little more grilling from the Peanut Gallery, mom tried to tiptoe around the downside of the new vocation. "It will be shift work," she said, covering her mouth as if to jumble the announcement. Translation—one month on days, one month on evenings and one month on nights—a new shift every thirty days. Uneasiness began to set in as I glumly realized that mom would not be available for supper nor to say 'goodnight' to most of the time. The upside, that I could practically run wild when she was on those shifts, seemed muted and almost anti-climactic.

Then came the worst aspect of mom's new job. She would provide few details about her responsibilities other than to say that her work station was on the "110 Line" and she would be "handling" fuses. Soon enough, though, she revealed that she would be part of an assembly team that installed fuses in the subcomponents of cluster bombs. The employer might have been Day & Zimmerman, but they only managed the plant that she would be working in. The facility was owned by the government and was a weapons manufacturing facility. With the war in 'Nam raging, business was apparently good. Good enough to hire a down-but-not-out mother of three—soon to be four—whose previous employment high water mark was serving up chilled Hamm's Beer to the glassy-eyed dead-enders at E&M Tavern.

The thought of my mother assembling and installing fuses in cluster bombs bound for Southeast Asia and the Ho Chi Minh Trail, the threat of explosion and death ever-present, made me want to improve in school and start saying prayers every night. Funny how the spectre of the imminent death of a loved one can cause one to re-examine his or her priorities. To be sure, there seemed to be a lot of stuff coming at me during this time—mom's pregnancy, going through the hormonal gates of puberty hell, and now the bomb factory shell shocker.

On top of it all, in November of that year, mom, with virtually no fanfare, kicked new hubby and father Bill out of the house and filed for divorce—all before delivering our newest sibling. This was all very troubling but not altogether unexpected. No reason for the ouster was given, but she did divulge that he had only spent one week living with her in our home. That was one week more than I had seen him.

Still, the thought of my 35 year old mother facing child birth alone and without support—and then having to return to the assembly line—was enough to make me consider running away to join the circus. Then I was reminded that I didn't have to run away to join it. Hell, I was in it—and one of the main attractions at that.

It should be no surprise that I was totally unprepared for the arrival of my new brother. Mom delivered without incident and brought Tim home exactly one week before Christmas 1968 on a frigid day replete with snow showers. In the spirit of the season we nicknamed him "Tiny Tim" and did our best to welcome him to our dysfunctional family. The only one who seemed unconcerned about the middle-of-the-night crying and odorous diaper pails was Bodie, our white Persian cat. He was named after Jethro Bodine of *The Beverly Hillbillies* TV show and had only slightly more common sense than his namesake. He disdainfully sniffed Tim on occasion and always walked away with his head in the air, supremely confident of his role in the now-chaotic household.

One of the many ways I dealt with the stresses that winter was to partner up with Donnie and Jason in the snow shoveling business. To adequately fund our voracious appetite for chili cones and spud nuts, it became necessary to enter the work world—at least to a point where our school work was not impacted. Not that our grades couldn't have gotten much worse.

While most neighborhood kids spent those snowy days sledding down South Ashby Street hill or skating on a frozen Santa Fe Lake, we trudged door-to-door, shovels over our shoulders, hang-dog looks on our faces. Whatever we did, it seemed to work as we never had a shortage of drives and sidewalks to clear.

Our most loyal and indefatigable customer was elderly widower Mrs. Pendarvis. She was also the most logistically friendly as she lived just across the street from the Hildebrandt's in a crumbling two-story house whose interior smelled of Vicks Vap-O-Rub and spilled cough syrup. She lived with her deaf sister and so always seemed excited to have someone to talk to who could actually hear.

Kind to a fault, she could always be counted on for leaf raking in the fall, snow removal in the winter and mowing in the summer. And in between the seasonal jobs, the demure spinster perpetually seemed to have any number of projects that involved moving heavy furniture, retrieving items from extraordinarily high places and re-arranging yard art.

Without fail, she would offer up hot tea and home-made chocolate chip cookies as a stipend to the completion of our work. She loved to talk about "the old days," and her recall of an America gone by was my introduction into nostalgia—odd that it was for a time in history that I was not a part of. Her gentle, effacing demeanor had a profound effect on me and made me realize that not all old folks were bitter, cantankerous, spiteful of youth and needing to be herded into a retirement home. We always shoveled and raked and mowed her property just a little better than all of the others as our way of paying respect.

The little house on South Grant Street where we lived was cramped and small for a young mother and her four children. Older sis had her own room, little sis and I shared a room with a bunk bed and Tiny Tim spent his first few months in mom's bedroom—another converted dining room—with its window facing the calamitous din of the railroad yard. How he slept at all with the banging of boxcars and grinding throttle of road switchers is beyond me. I guess, like the rest of us, he probably and quickly developed a defense mechanism that reduced the clamoring to a backdrop of white noise.

One of the positive changes that working in a bomb factory did for mom was to rid her of dependency on relief and food stamps for survival. I knew that she secretly abhorred having to enroll us on the reduced lunch program at school and having to send us to the store with those dreaded booklets that screamed "we're poor!" Perhaps only she hated it worse than me.

Still, it was refreshing to know that there were still good and virtuous people left in the world in the troubling year of 1968. One of those individuals was a grocer named Jeff Cates. He was the thin, bespectacled and friendly proprietor and owner of Jeff's Foodliner, the closest grocery store to our little home. To open the door and step into his establishment at the corner of Main and Grant was to lurch back firmly in time. Except for the air conditioned coolness and the goods, nothing, it seemed, had changed for about 35 years.

The narrow plank wood floors creaked and groaned with every customer step. Ceiling fans, hung from the expansive tin ceiling, whirred contentedly. The old style cash registers rang (literally) with delight. Every employee, even the ones in the meat department, beamed broadly at every turn. Though it sat squarely on Main Street, Jeff's Foodliner had the look and feel of an old country store that would have been more comfortable, perhaps, on an old back road far out in the boondocks.

Best of all, he extended credit to some customers—my mom included—who might not otherwise have been able to eat regularly. And he delivered. This was especially helpful to our still car-less family, even though we only lived 2 blocks from his store. The sight of that old Plymouth station wagon ambling up into our driveway on any given Saturday afternoon was a most welcome sight. The whole interior of the old clunker, excepting the driver's seat, was filled with sacks brimming with groceries.

It was almost like Christmas—only it happened virtually every week instead of once a year.

Based on mom's newfound wealth risking life and limb on a regular basis, we were soon able to afford some luxuries that were heretofore unheard of. One of those indulgences was air conditioning—sort of. Up until that point in our lives, the only conditioned air that any of us had ever experienced came when we visited some of the stores downtown that had it—including Zip Drug, A& P Grocery, Jeff's and any of the department stores. My aunt and uncle and cousins in Wichita, where we visited every summer, also had a wonderful old window a/c unit that absolutely blasted chilled air throughout their modest brick rancher.

You could hang meat in their living room. I swear.

I guess it was only a matter of time that we would get one of our own, too. Little did I know that the unit we were getting was *used* and not an air conditioner in the literal sense. Unloading it one humid spring day, I overheard one of the deliverymen refer to it as a "swamp cooler" or "water cooler." In fact it was an evaporative cooler—most effectively used in climates where the temperatures are hot and the humidity is low. Problem was that our humidity levels in Southeast Kansas tended to be on the high side during spring and summer.

That fact made the purchase a most curious one.

The only thing I could think of was that mom must have got the monstrosity on sale and had it shipped from some desert locale such as Arizona or New Mexico. It was the size of a large refrigerator and was already showing signs of red rust. No matter, though. Once the water line was connected, the juice flowing and the fan was humming, everything—and I mean everything—in the house got damp and cool very quickly. I learned to avoid sitting on the couch lest I get up with a wet butt. The throw rugs squished beneath our feet. And, in what might have been the most plausible explanation of how the cooling device got its nickname, soon enough our whole house smelled like a freshwater Louisiana swamp.

All in all, though, I guess it was better than the hot old days when all we had was one small and lousy box fan with its wheezing motor and frayed electrical cord.

Caught up more and more in the slipstream pressures of junior high school, my delinquent friends and disorderly home life, I turned inward at times for remedies to a malaise that I could not properly define. After laboring rather clumsily for a couple of years at the paint-by-number kits that mom bought for 'special' occasions, I finally decided that I could do better on my own.

Of course that meant purchasing from Orr's Color Center little tubes of Grumbacher oil paint in every conceivable color, linseed oil, canvasses, camel hair brushes, an easel and virtually everything else the starter book recommended to foaming-at-the-mouth novices. I was inspired by the illustrations I had seen, particularly those of Paul Detlefsen, in Tiny Tim's babysitter's collection of *Ideals* magazine. She loaned them to me by the dozens and I was fascinated by the Americana awash on every page. I often wondered if Mrs. Pendarvis had a subscription. She would surely appreciate the tranquil scenes of bucolic schoolhouses, dirt roads trodden by horse-drawn buggies and blacksmith shops nestled in leafy dells.

So too was I incentivized by the large sofa paintings of the likes of Robert Wood. Johnson's Furniture Store on East Main Street had a number of them hanging on their walls high above a menagerie of poster beds, Barcaloungers, blonde wood dresser drawers and armoires. I am not sure why, but I was curiously drawn to his intricately detailed landscapes of fallow mountain meadows, thick forests and bugling elks. Like Detlefesen, who took me back into a time in America that I had not known, Wood transported me to the wild Rocky Mountains of Colorado and the Grand Tetons of Wyoming that I had never seen. And perhaps might not ever see.

In any case, I am sure the Johnsons were perplexed by the sight of a 13 year old boy standing in the middle of their grand furniture store staring agape at the Wood's reproductions hanging on their walls. If so, they were gracious enough to never inquire or prod. Perhaps they knew by looking at me, with my tattered jeans and holy tennis shoes, that I wasn't there to purchase a new club chair and ottoman. No, I was there for inspiration.

I painted fast and furious that first year—far outpacing my ability to fund new canvas and paints. Over time I learned to slow down and take my time. It was just the medicine, I determined, to treat what had been ailing me. Whether I had enough talent to end up in the glossy interior of *Ideals* or on the wall in some future furniture store clearly remained to be seen, though.

Of course, sitting at an easel painting idyllic vistas could not hide me from everyone whom I desired to evade, so I eventually discovered a secret place where I could be completely alone. It was so clever, so right-under-their-nose that to this day I have to laugh and pat myself on the back.

Our house on South Grant Street had a very curious design. It was nearly square and had four flat corners of a roof that came to a point in the middle and at a slope just gentle enough to scale. Getting to the flat corner to be able to scale the final peak was the problem. However, I soon found a way up via the breezeway between our garage and the neighbor's garage to the south. The narrow corridor was elevated to the point that I could, with some difficulty, shimmy up on our garage roof. Once their, I had to scale down the north side of the garage roof and leap across to the southwest flat corner of the house roof. From their I side-stepped all the way up to the top of the roof.

When I wanted to get lost, that is where I went. The Drifters "Up On the Roof" became my own personal theme song whose every note I held dearly. It was quite serene on a hot summer night, for instance, to watch bats swarm out of the drainage canal—which ran directly underneath our house—at dusk to pick off all of the flying insects that buzzed the railroad yard light across the street. Yes, the very same yard light where we had ill-advisedly hurled Drooper to his death months earlier.

For some reason, I enjoyed the contrast of not being able to be found yet right there at home—not to mention the moon and stars and the sounds of the city fading into night. It was possible, for instance, to hear on the same night the sonic boom of the crashing rail cars and numberless crickets symphonizing in perfect harmony in the pipe yard to the north of our house. Those serendipitous benefits always made the trip up to the top of the roof wonderfully worthwhile—and the trip down just a little melancholy.

One of the things that I did not see from my lofty perch was the arrival and departure of The Oil Flyer, one of Santa Fe's two Kansas City-Tulsa daily passenger trains that served Chanute. The venerable train was deemed unprofitable by Santa Fe's management, agreed to by the ICC and thus removed from service right before we moved to our new location, leaving only The Tulsan to ply the route. In a year of change—a virtual sea of change—the death of the Oil Flyer, a train I had never ridden on, was an ominous precursor for me. What was next? The Greyhound Bus? Telephone service? Never mind that we did not have a telephone either.

In the Summer of 1968 I learned through the kid grapevine that my two old buddies, Darren and Charles, had moved with their families out of town. Darren's dad had sold his bakery and moved the entire family to Tulsa, OK—some 150 miles to the south. It might as well have been Ethiopia. There was no doubt that I would never see Darren again.

Charles' mom found a new, better paying job in a small western Missouri town and they had left virtually overnight. Leaving no relatives behind in Chanute, it was literally assured that I would never see him again, either. Though I had not been in close contact with either of them in a while, the loss of two of my old Alcott friends was felt with a dull pang of despair. A part of my young past was now irrevocably torn away and discarded.

My new friends, ever creative when it came to finding new ways to get into trouble, carried on with me in tow. For some bizarre reason only the city fathers and local law enforcement officials could explain, there was a curfew in Chanute in 1968 that forbade anyone under 16 years of age to be on the streets after 10:00 PM. This generally wasn't a problem, excepting Friday and Saturday nights—and summer.

The ruse was simple, time-worn and far from elaborate. I told my mom I was spending the night with Jason. Jason told his dad that he was spending the night with Donnie. And Donnie, of course, told his parents that he was spending the night with me. Which meant all of us were free to roam the city's streets all night—providing we could avoid detection by the gendarmes. That usually involved diving into bushes, running down alleys, ducking behind cars and carrying stealth to new and previously unimagined heights.

It is truly miraculous that we were never caught, given some of the nocturnal activities we indulged in. One of our favorites was making our way out to the far south side of town to a place called Kart-Wheel. Paying customers could, during normal business hours, jump on the trampolines, play a round of mini-golf or brave the dangerous go-kart track. Naturally, this was a must-stop on the after hours tour for us. The fence surrounding the facility was no match for us and we scaled it with virtually no effort.

While we never summoned up the courage to fire up any of the go-karts for a midnight ride, we did have some memorable moments on the trampolines. The most fun, I have to admit, was laying flat and trying to remain perfectly still as one of the night beat cops drove through and, following protocol, shone his flashlight around from inside the air-conditioned comfort of his cruiser. It was a curious blend of euphoria and terror that pulsed through my veins as his light scanned over the top of our heads. We were up and jumping again before his taillights were completely out of sight.

Though tame by contrast to some of the things kids get into nowadays, I have always felt a tincture of guilt for jumping on the trampolines without paying. On the days when we had enough money to ride the go-karts, I always wanted to overpay the operators. Then again, there were always more tubes of Cadmium Red and Number 2 brushes to buy.

If I now feel bad for my transgressions at Kart-Wheel, I am completely loathe to divulge that we also went for a few late night swims at the city pool. I state this out of my complete reverence for the whole Maring family and the fact that they let my sisters and I swim for free on a number of occasions. It just seemed so cool, so forbidden to have the pool all to ourselves and the moonlight.

To top it all off, scaling the 8-foot high chain-link fence was every bit the challenge that Kart-Wheel's was not. And when the flatfoots did make their rounds by the pool, we had to be careful to not ripple the water or make any noise. Trust me; it is much more difficult to calm water than a trampoline. Most of the time, we slid silently underwater, resurfacing only when we were certain that the coast was clear. Then came the same ying and yang brew of elation and fright that had coursed through my veins at the trampolines. Only the guilt made it far worse.

Up until my 8th grade year, the extent of my education about sex consisted of privately ogling naked African tribal women in *National Geographic* magazine at the public library, perusing the women's lingerie section of the Montgomery Ward sale catalogue, exchanging bold faced lies with Donnie and Jason about our most recent conquests and thumbing through my Uncle Al's copy of *Monsieur* that I stole from his barn one year earlier. Then two incidents occurred at school that, temporarily at least, jarred my sensibilities regarding the opposite sex.

The rumor spread through the halls of Royster Junior High like a wind-whipped Flinthills fire. A 9th grader had a large, lewd photograph of a naked woman and he was going to display it in the boy's breezeway bathroom at 12:15. The timing worked out great for me, as my lunch period began at 12:00 sharp. I would just need to eat rather hurriedly and then head over to the commons area that separated the classrooms and administration from the big and little gymnasiums.

Out of the crowded, noisy cafeteria by ten minutes after, I arrived on time for the big show only to find a long line of boys shuffling slowly forward in a human chain that seemed to stretch to Kansas City. It was an odd scene as that particular restroom was virtually uninhabited most of the time during the day. Now several boys would come out and several more would go in—sort of like a revolving door without the ability to revolve. I panned the crowd not only to seek out familiar faces but to also take note of the expressions of those waiting to go in as well as those emerging from the show. None of my closest friends were in the lineup, though I recognized many fellow 8th graders.

As I stood fidgeting in line, it occurred to me that there were a couple of scenarios, should they unfold, that might doom my chances to see an actual naked girl—or at least a photograph of an actual naked girl that wasn't holding a spear or who didn't look like Ernest Borgnine. The exhibitor might have to get back to class, thereby shutting down the display before I got there. Or Principal Parsons might see the unusual serpentine line of boys jostling to get in a usually empty bathroom and haul us all off to the abyss of the Guidance Counselor.

Either way, I was starting to get nervous. Still, I had come this far and there was no backing down now. Not even the confused, perplexed stares of 9th grade girls passing by on their way to gym class could deter me from my date with a photo of an unnamed naked girl. I just hoped it was an 8"X10" or larger format—and in glorious color.

Not nearly soon enough, my turn to enter the portal of obscenity finally came. To say that it was anticlimactic would be an understatement. If I had paid for the privilege, I would have most assuredly asked for a refund. The photograph was that of an older woman—not a girl—and it was in black and white, not color. And though it did show more of the female body than any of the models shown in the nudie magazine I had stolen, I decided that there were some things—especially at this young age—that should wait to be seen. This was definitely one of them.

Dejected, I came forth from the bathroom feeling as if I were an unobservant tourist whose pockets had just been picked on a Paris cobblestone. However disappointing this incident might have been to me and the 200 other boys who risked their reputations to stand in line, what followed in the next week took the proverbial cake.

In 8th grade at that time, boys were required to take physical education and health education as part of their curriculum. Along the way, some administrative guru decided that it would be to our advantage to have the PE classes on Monday, Wednesday and Friday of every week and have the HE on Tuesdays and Thursdays.

Like the bathroom naked girl fiasco, it all started with a rumor the size of Texas. The very last HE class of the school year was coming up and whispers that it involved film of a naked girl made it to virtually every 8th grade boys ears. "What kind of film?" I naturally and quizzically asked of one of my peers. "Is she a dancer? What kind of film could they possibly show that would include footage of a naked girl?"

No one seemed to really know, but it was a sure bet that there would be, for the first time ever, 100% attendance in all of the HE classes that day.

I had health education 2nd hour that year, so any news from the front—the 1st hour boys—did not reach my command post before I was to report to class. Not knowing what to expect, other than a naked girl on film, I trudged off to the trade building to further and enlighten my knowledge of the health and well-being of the fairer sex.

In retrospect, it was probably a good thing that none of the 1st hour survivors were able to extrapolate what they saw that fateful spring morning. As the classroom swelled with anxious film lovers, and before the lights were lowered, we were given a brief introduction by our instructor of its content. It would be, he informed us with a gravely serious look, a "graphic visual compendium of the birth of a child."

Oh, yeah.

Then the door was closed, the room darkened and the projector began to whirr. There was dialogue in the film, but to this day I cannot remember one line of it. The very first image, however, was unforgettable. For starters, the woman about to give birth looked eerily similar to the naked chick in the bathroom photo. Seeing any of the girls in *Monsieur* would have been an improvement.

In my young life I had never witnessed a naked woman strapped in stirrups on a medical gurney before. By the way my classmates reacted, I'm pretty sure that no one else in the room had either. The cinematographer should have been given an Oscar for the way he trained his camera on her most private parts—and for at least the moment the film critics were in vacuous approval.

Soon enough, though, the crowning began and the baby's head started to appear from between her legs. One by one, you could see the nonplussed expressions begin to wash over the faces of the startled crowd. At this point, I will spare the reader most of the gory details, but let's just say that there was in short order, besides a baby, the expelling of the placenta and membranes of the fetus. Oh, and there was blood—lots of it.

At this point, some of my classmates had their heads down on their desk, unable to look at the carnage anymore. Others were upright in their seats, but had their eyes closed, as if doing so would make it all go away. At the very front of the room, friend John Bowes fainted dead away and had to be pulled across the floor to the safety of the hallway outside. I was reminded of old, grainy war footage where a fallen soldier is carried by his comrades to protection, bombs exploding all around.

I wanted to yell out "we surrender," and wave the white flag but it was too late.

To this day, I am convinced that, rather than the health education film school officials touted it as, it was actually an anti-sex education film. No boy who witnessed that twenty-minute horror film could honestly say that he would still have sex with a woman. The administrators and instructors knew it, too. Teachers 1, boys 0.

The bell finally, gratefully rang ending our persecution. It would be months before I could get some of the lurid images out of my head. Sex would, at least for the time being, be left to the adults of the world to contemplate and deal with.

Among the many suitors that came to call on my mom over the years, Gene Morton was perhaps my very favorite. He was short and muscular, fatally honest and hardworking—and he treated my mother like a princess. They met in one of the numerous Chanute watering holes and only dated for a brief time. He lived in a little shanty by the railroad tracks just a few blocks from us and worked at the refinery at the north end of town.

He was raising, by himself, a son two years younger than me. That meant that I got to go with them on fishing trips to area farm ponds, Saturday afternoons at the carnival without selling pop bottles to pay for the rides and an occasional 'boys night' at the Morton house. For some reason, the romance fizzled—at least on mom's part—and finally came to an end almost before it started. Naturally this was disconcerting news.

Not nearly as unsettling as the news we received one sultry early spring night in 1969, though. Not long after the split, Gene was operating a tractor mower at the plant and on a particularly hilly section of the grounds, the tractor tipped over, pinning and crushing him to death. Of all of the things I had experienced in our family over the years, dealing with such loss was not among them.

Gene was the first person to die that I knew personally, and his passing was a seminal moment in my life. Mom could not bring herself to either attend the viewing nor the funeral. But as I had a good relationship with Gene and often saw him as a father figure—he was the first to teach me, for instance, how to fillet a fish—I decided to attend the viewing.

The walk to Gibson-Koch Chapel, where Gene's body lay in repose, was only about three blocks from our house. I put on my best dress shirt and slacks and headed to the funeral home. I remember it clearly because I walked alone and it was so incredibly hot—and I was sweating profusely under the long-sleeved shirt. The sun had disappeared beyond the western horizon and inky blackness was settling in.

Nervously, I signed the register and was directed to the room where Gene lay in his casket. I must have been the last of the visitors as there was no one else around. It was just me and Gene in the dimly lit and eerie stillness. I was startled to see that he was dressed in a suit and tie—like a sleeping businessman with bad make-up. As I had never seen him in anything but jeans or chinos and tee shirts, he did not look real. This fact really bothered me because I *wanted* him to look like him.

I closed my eyes and said a quiet prayer for the man I admired but never really got to know. And then I headed out the door for home—my head swirling with questions about death and dying. There was so much that I did not know. What happens to us when we die? Where do we go? I hoped Gene was in Heaven making his famous chocolate chip pancakes.

One thing I did know, however—life could end at any time in any fashion. This was naturally a sobering assessment for one who had never experienced loss of this type.

As the decade neared its final year, the winds of change were definitely and with ever-growing force blowing through my little town—and my little family. Some things would never be the same—thankfully on one hand and regrettably on the other.

GOING LIGHTLY FROM THE LEDGE

Summer was but a few days old in 1969 when mom, Deirdre and I loaded up in Uncle Marlon's station wagon for our annual trip to Wichita. Older sister Margaret stayed behind to tend to babysitting responsibilities. The hum of that well-worn ribbon of a highway that led, much like the entrance to the Emerald City, to the sprawling metropolis, was a lullaby that rocked me gently to sleep—in broad daylight, no less. Scarcely had we stepped out of the big, white schooner at my cousin's house than the itinerary for the week was meticulously laid out before us.

One of the first things on the list was an afternoon swim in the neighborhood pool, Country Acres, just a few short blocks from our cousin's modest blonde brick rancher. The pool, owned and operated by the City of Wichita, looked banal enough at first glance, with its sparkling, clear water, impressive diving boards, concrete bath house and freshly painted life guard stations. The landscaping around the structure was meticulous and well-kept.

The first sign that something wasn't quite right came when, upon arrival at midday, I noticed only a few swimmers in the water. The majority of the patrons were lying in the sun, sitting and talking or eating at the snack bar. "Oh, yeah," my cousin Sherry Anne said to me, almost as an afterthought, "Country Acres is supposedly the coldest public pool in Wichita."

"It can't be that cold," I shot back, confident that once I got in the water the masses would surely follow. I'm here to report that they didn't. I made the decision to dive in, thinking that if I waded slowly in I might be forced to make a hasty, cowardly retreat. There was no backing out of a head-first dive. And dive I did.

It was cold, all right. In fact, water swirling around ice floes would have been warmer. The only things missing were Emperor Penguins and icebreaking tugs. Red hot needles shot through every part of my body that was submerged in the glacial pool. Icicles began to form on the tips of my hair. I turned blue and began to go numb, and recognizing the early stages of hypothermia, began to feebly swim back to the safety of a service ladder.

"I told you it was going to be cold," I thought I heard Sherry Anne snicker. I couldn't hear out of my right ear from the slush build-up. I would have punched her, too, but I couldn't lift either of my arms up. They were now frozen in the down position at my side. All I could do was whimper. Where once I had been excited to get the chance to go to a new and different public pool—one probably teeming with new and exotic girls—I now lay curled up in a fetal position on my towel cursing my cousin through purple lips.

I could hardly wait for the next Wichita adventure.

As luck would have it, I didn't have to wait long. The next day we loaded up the wagon and headed for Joyland, a small amusement park located in south Wichita. Though it had just celebrated its 20th birthday a week earlier, the place had a slightly tawdry look and quirky ambiance that made it feel much older. It had all of the trappings of great adventure—a miniature gauge steam locomotive pulled smiley-faces around the park on a gently curving track, a real wooden roller coaster loomed up from the distance, the smell of fresh cotton candy filled the air and the sounds of laughing children permeated the air. Still, there was a sinister undercurrent that I couldn't quite shake out of my head.

It didn't help that the first thing we did was wolf down a year's supply of undercooked hot dogs, stale popcorn and root beer. Next stop—The Rollercoaster. I couldn't believe that Joyland's anchor ride—the heart and soul of the park, if you will—had no name. It was just called "The Rollercoaster." How lame, I thought. "So this is the big, bad rollercoaster that you all have been talking about?" I asked my cousin, rolling my eyes in disbelief. I had heard all of the horror stories, but now that it was within sight, it looked demonstrably less intimidating.

"It's scarier than it looks," she assured me. At that moment, I should have remembered her warnings about the water temperature at Country Acres. Doubtfully, I trudged ahead of the rest of the group to the coaster approach, where the line was surprisingly short. The Rollercoaster was a classic 'out-and-back' design that featured a 2,600' track span and an 80' drop that propelled its victims to a top speed of 50 mph. The wooden beams and cross-members were painted a bright white. I heard the faint creaking and moaning of the timbers as the coaster snaked over the rails overhead. I began to worry just ever so slightly.

Still, droves of disembarked riders were laughing hysterically at the exit end of the canopy. How bad could it be? I was about to find out.

The toboggan cars were of the lap-bar type and seemed a tad insecure for my tastes. Yet I somewhat reluctantly plopped down with little sis beside me in a car near the middle of the pack, smiling like a man whistling past the graveyard. At this point I have to inform the reader that I had never previously been on a rollercoaster in my life. The most thrilling rides I had ever experienced to that point in my young life were the Ferris Wheel and Tilt-O-Whirl at the local carnivals. That was about to change.

Little sis and I got in one car and Sherry Anne jumped in the one behind us. Then the skid brakes and anti-rollback gears were released and the coaster began its arduous, clanking climb up to the first—and highest—drop. It was a beautiful, cloudless day and I gaped in wonderment at the view as we climbed ever higher above the trees. People down below turned into ants on a picnic table. The music and laughter began to fade under the sounds of the coaster laboring up the incline—and the wind which was now whipping furiously.

Near the summit we passed under a sign that read "Last Warning: Do Not Stand Up. Sit Down." My last thought before the cars catapulted over the precipice was "wow, people have to be *warned* to not stand up." Hell, I couldn't get down *low* enough. As we went over the edge I looked out over the horizon that didn't seem to stop and thought I saw our house 113 miles away.

We careened madly down the first drop and then back up and over a second rise. My face was contorted in a grotesque G-force induced mask of joy and terror. It was probably also a nice shade of green from the food consumed just a few minutes earlier that was threatening to come back up. "Please God," I prayed, "don't let me throw up on my sister."

"Sherry Anne, maybe, but not my sister…"

Like a stray bullet, the coaster wheeled through the dogleg turnaround and over a few more slightly less intimidating bunny hops before it cruised, floated actually, into the station. The first thing I did was check to see if I had soiled myself. Then I looked to see if sis had made it back. She had. We were all full of vim and vinegar after having conquered The Rollercoaster.

"Wanna ride it again?" Sherry Anne asked, excitedly.

"Maybe later," I offered, puffing out my chest just a little. "Let's go see what else there is to do in this place."

We ended up riding most of the rides, even the Paratrooper and Round Up, but the most terrifying thing in the amusement park turned out to *not* be a ride at all. Joyland had a most curious attraction, an old Wurlitzer pipe organ, built in 1905 and situated near the epicenter of the park. Military band sounds resonated throughout the grounds from the old organ and like children flocking to a pied piper, we found our way to it.

As we got closer to the organ, I noticed a clown playing it. "He's not real," Sherry Anne explained. "He's automated and his name is Louie." Sure enough, Louie was a mechanical clown who stiffly plied the keys of the old steam organ with his back to an adoring public. There was a sign at the bottom of his chair that warned "Do not talk to operator." I noted that there seemed to be an abundance of 'do not' signs at the park.

But after getting a close-up look at his creepy face with its fixed grin and empty, soulless eyes, I could see why one shouldn't be talking to Louie.

Louie's eerie face reminded me immediately of Conrad Veidt's character Gwynplaine in the 1928 silent film *The Man Who Laughs* in which his face is disfigured, as punishment for offending English nobility in 1690, into a permanent rictus grin by King James' surgeon.

I had nightmares about Louie showing up and tapping at my bedroom window in the moonlight for months after that. Louie was in my closet. Louie was in our darkened garage. Louie was inside my head.

"Let's do something else," I said to Sherry Anne. "Louie gives me the heebie jeebies. Do any of the food trailers here serve chili cones?"

"What's a chili cone?" she asked with a look of sincere consternation. I should have known better.

Our time in Wichita, as it usually did, flew by, and soon we were careening back across the Flint Hills toward home where mom would resume making bombs and little sis and I would go back to hanging out with our friends. It was the last time we would ever make the annual summer trip to Wichita again as a group. Events occurring within both families in the coming year would bring to an end one of the most memorable hallmarks of summers in my youth.

Back home and in the bad company of Jason and Donnie, our newest challenge became the search for an older classmate with a car who could take us "dragging Main." Dragging Main was the local idiom for driving one's car mindlessly back and forth, from east to west, on Main Street, Chanute's principal street. As it was very much a social event, we were hopelessly out of touch and rarely found anyone who would haul us around—except for Melvin.

As long as we had money for gas, Melvin was only too eager to have us along. But even us societal outsiders had scruples and felt a pang of embarrassment climbing into—and being seen in—his cancer-riddled Fairlane. We affectionately nicknamed his hulk "The Bug Sprayer" for the plume of blue smoke that trailed behind it on those forays up and down Main Street. Dragging Main did little for us other than strengthen the notion that one of us needed to step up on our 16th birthday (the earliest non-farm age that you could legally drive in Kansas in 1969) and get a car so that we could stop relying on Melvin.

In preparation, I suppose, for that future day when we would have our own clunker, I began an eclectic little habit of collecting road maps from all of the local gas stations. From Boyer's Apco to Dale's Skelly Service to Washburn Texaco out on North Santa Fe, I hit them all. The station attendants always seemed mystified why a 14-year old boy would need a road map of Iowa or Wisconsin. "It's a long way there on a bike," the counterman from Rich's Derby sarcastically informed me one day, eyeing my dilapidated Sting-ray.

"They're for my mom," I shot back, grabbing maps of Missouri, Nebraska and Kansas off the display rack and stuffing them in my jeans pocket. "She has a new Oldsmobile Toronado," I added for emphasis. "It has front wheel drive, ya know?"

"Get outta here, kid," he muttered, and in a flash I was gone with the entire Midwest atlas in my possession. I made a mental note to crash my first car through the plate glass window of the Derby station specifically on any night he worked.

For a little, sleepy Midwestern town, Chanute boasted a vibrant and engaging music scene in the later part of the decade. Bud Ross, a local entrepreneur, founded Kustom Electronics in 1966 to manufacture and market his line of guitar and bass amplifiers. Kustom Amps were unique in their appearance—mass produced in tuck-and-roll Naugahyde—and were favored in the day by some of the most popular bands.

Groups such as The Yardbirds, Sam the Sham & the Pharaohs, Gary Lewis and the Playboys, Creedence Clearwater Revival and Tommy James and the Shondells would roll into town to demo, purchase and pick up equipment—and sometimes end up playing a concert for the locals before departing to bigger and better venues.

There were even a few local bands—namely The Sensational Showmen and The Common Few?—who played all of the local armories and Eagles' Halls to the delight of rabid followers and star-struck teens. All of this was fed and fueled, of course, by the incessant pounding of Top 40 hits from WHB AM-71 Radio in Kansas City. The World's Happiest Broadcasters kept shoveling the coals that drove the musical engine.

Chanute was also the birthplace and boyhood home of Paul Lindblad, a left-handed flamethrower who by 1969 was playing with the Oakland Athletics and would enjoy his finest year as a Major League Baseball player. He had grown up and played ball at all of the local diamonds and sandlots and seemed destined for stardom. While many of us kids were resentful that swashbuckler owner Charlie "O" Finley, despite his continual assurances to the contrary, moved the Athletics from Kansas City to Oakland in 1968, Lindblad made it easier to root for the green and gold. He was one of us.

I even became somewhat of a local celebrity for a brief time in the Summer of 1969. Not so much for my musical or baseball abilities, but for my knowledge of Chanute history. KCRB AM at 1460 on the dial was our own little radio station where hog futures, swap and shop and forgettable music (at least for a 14-year old) were usually the order of the day. KCRB did, for a brief time, hold a daily contest whereby if one correctly answered a question about the city's history, the reward came in the form of a six-pack of Mountain Dew.

Naturally, the idea of answering easy questions to get free soda pop spurred me on to new intellectual heights. It wasn't long before I had a couple of cases of the stuff stored out on the back porch. I won so much and so often that KCRB eventually put the kibosh on me, limiting the number of times any one listener could win. I felt as if I were being punished for my intricate knowledge of my hometown. It was also the first time I realized how much better free stuff tasted.

Summer rolled on and we often found ourselves on clear and pleasant mornings at Santa Fe Lake, fishing off of the large rock outcroppings that peppered the east shoreline. There, between baiting hooks and diving into the water from the small cliffs, we debated long-held rumors that a railroad engine and some gondolas lay at the bottom of the lake—victims of a collapsed spur bridge.

Never mind that the Santa Fe Railroad had never constructed a bridge over the lake.

And in what was surely a new twist to an old legend, it was also reputed that Water Moccasins had built large nests in the submersed wreckage and were poised to attack and bite any swimmer that dove too deep.

Never mind that Water Moccasins were not indigenous to the area. It was not uncommon to see a Copperhead tangoing on the surface of the sun-dappled water, though.

Then there was the Warwick Wax Plant across the lake to the west, an apocalyptic-looking petrochemical plant whose stacks plumed with acrid smoke to the accompaniment of the sounds of machinery hissing and grinding. We were not sure what kind of wax was being produced there, but we were pretty sure that they were not making candles like the ones we fashioned in grade school art class. The sprawling, foreboding complex was only accessible by a service road near the railroad tracks. From the cliffs on the east side of the lake it looked like a haunted island with its very own crematorium.

"Maybe they make wax figures for museums," Jason intoned. We all looked at each other with nervous grins. "Well, it's possible," he reasoned.

We briefly entertained the idea of trying to gain access to the plant via a canoe or fishing boat. Then, in a rare moment of clarity and reason, we decided against it. The foul smell of the acid sludge burial pits and the clanging of engaging gears and conveyors invoked just enough fear in our hearts to stamp out even the most ardent bravado. The wax plant would forever remain a mystery to us.

On July 20th Neil Armstrong and Buzz Aldrin walked on the moon. I watched the grainy footage beamed live from a camera mounted in the Lunar Module from the Hildebrandt's living room couch. The room reeked of popcorn and Estee Lauder, Mrs. Hildebrandt's favorite perfume. History was made a second time that night when all eleven Hildebrandts sat together at once and in shocked, rare silence in front of the TV. We had fulfilled President Kennedy's promise and beaten the Russians. It was a great time to be an American.

After watching our flag being planted on the surface of the moon, we went outside and shot all of the rest of our unused fireworks from the 4th. Across the street, Mrs. Pendarvis pulled her front window curtains to one side and peered nervously out in our direction. "We're on the moon!" I screamed, twirling a sparkler. She smiled, waved feebly and disappeared from the window. At that moment I wondered how she, alive during the time of horse-drawn carriages and gas lamps, felt about seeing a man step foot on a celestial body 239,000 miles away from Earth.

The euphoria of that moment lasted until well into the night when we fell asleep on the screened-in porch of the Hildebrandt house to the concerto murmur of crickets, beetles and frogs.

Always on the lookout for new fishing holes, we were given a tip from a pro in late July that the Bullhead were biting beneath Austin Bridge on the Neosho River southeast of the city. None of us had actually fished there before, so early one hazy morning we gathered up all of the angling accouterments we owned and set out for the river.

To get there, we followed the ATSF Railroad's branch line to Pittsburg as it meandered east. At a point just a mile or so south of the city dump, the line intersected with the Missouri-Kansas-Texas branch line to Parsons. There we followed the "Katy" south all of the way to the outskirts of the unincorporated and nearly abandoned village of Austin.

By 1969 all that was left of the once vibrant river town were a few ramshackle houses and a scattering of old, rusting hulks that had once been cars. Weeds and noxious grasses were strangling the last breath of life out of sidewalks, front yards and out buildings. Everything, it seemed, was either dead or dying in Austin. It's only impressive feature remained the expansive bowstring through truss bridge high over the muddy Neosho on the eastern edge of town. Built in 1872 by the King Iron Bridge Company, it was still in use but looking, like its namesake city, rather worse for the wear.

Rot had eaten large, gaping holes in the planks—and even the two wooden runners for car tires were showing signs of extreme wear on the 160-foot long structure. Down below, the river flowed lazily out of a long, deep pool to a series of riffles and sandbars. On the east bank of the tributary columns of large Cottonwood trees rustled noisily in the wind, competing with the rapids for auditory prominence.

We set up camp that morning and proceeded to pull all kinds of fish from the brown foam—Carp, Gar, Bullhead, Channel Cat and even a water snake. We didn't keep any of them, however, and ended up, as most of our fishing forays did, swimming and playing in the water. We also passed the time setting up shells as targets on large driftwood logs and competing to see who could shatter the most with river rocks.

Hiking out to Austin became a daily communion for us in the dog days summer of Sunflowers and lavender Thistles. Eventually we convinced the parents to let us all camp out there overnight and I can't tell you how invigorating it was to hear the coyotes yelp at night as we huddled close by a crackling riverside fire. We sat speechless underneath a canopy of a zillion stars that seemed so close you could touch them. The riffles were a lullaby that rocked us all to sleep after a long day of exploring, fishing and swimming.

All of this was a panacea to take our minds off the fact that we were not going to be able to go to the Woodstock Festival. Despite some fairly intricate, secret planning and hoarding of funds, it was finally decided that making the 1,385-mile journey to Yasgur's farm would be complicated by a lack of transportation—not to mention permission. So we spent the money collected for the music extravaganza on night crawlers and lures. We liked to joke that "Woodstock had Country Joe & the Fish; we had to settle for just the fish."

While throngs of hippie chicks and hip cats grooved to the beat of Sly & the Family Stone's "Hot Fun In the Summertime" on the stage in upstate New York, we were content to listen to it crackle out of Donnie's transistor radio on WHB over the din of the whistling Cottonwoods and rushing current. I am sure that we missed what would have been a milestone in our young lives by not going to Woodstock. Yet I can't help thinking how fortunate I was to have been in the company of good friends in nature's unhurried embrace at that particular moment in time.

To stagger home at the purple hue of dusk along the railroad tracks, desperately tired and smelling of fish, clothes wet and hanging from our bodies was a blessing and gift that we could not truly appreciate fully at the moment. To ride my bicycle home through the dark, silent streets after arriving back at the Hildebrandt's—minnow bucket strapped to my handlebars—was a yet unrealized endowment, a providence of youth.

Then, as it usually did, the real world sucker-punched us all in the face again.

On the night of August 8, actress Sharon Tate and four others in and near the Los Angeles home that she shared with famed director Roman Polanski were found brutally murdered. The next night, grocer Leno LaBianca and his wife Rosemary were likewise butchered and killed in their Los Feliz home. In both instances, the killers had scrawled words on the walls in their victim's blood. The murders were vile and despicable. Hardened investigators were mortified. The killings were so gruesome that people thousands of miles away from the scene of the crimes locked *their* doors.

We never experienced any murders in our home, but older sis did drop a bomb on the family in mid-August by getting married quietly and without fanfare to her boyfriend of one year. The elation of knowing that I would now have my own room co-mingled with the sadness that she was no longer going to be living in our house. In fact, she would be moving soon to her new hubby's hometown in western Kansas—literally a continent away. With mom still grinding out the swing shift and Tiny Tim doing the shuffle between babysitter's house and ours, it was left to little sis and I to survive on our own.

I quickly learned that she fixed a mean plate of fried potatoes. Unfortunately for the both of us, that was the extent of her culinary skills at the time.

I entered ninth grade, my final year, at Royster Junior High full of optimism—despite that fact that my grades were plankton and my social life, outside of Donnie and Jason and a few fringe outlanders, was pretty much non-existent. I vowed to change things for the better. Vows, I must now report, are much better suited for weddings.

By the first day of the new school year, our little group was practically subterranean. By that I mean that we were rarely seen outside of classes—and sometimes not there either, if we could help it. We wore a well-tread path down every back alley, unfenced yard, railroad right-of-way, foot path in the woods and parking lot in the city. We knew every shortcut to every destination—all without being seen on prominent streets and sidewalks. It was the twentieth century equivalent of living in the catacombs.

Shortly after Labor Day, the city hosted their very first Artist Alley, a festival where local citizens, skilled in creative activities, could display (and hopefully sell) their craft up and down a closed-off Main Street and in the alley's directly behind the stores. I was convinced, pushed actually, by friends and relatives to set up a booth to showcase my fine paintings. Despite getting a primo spot in front of a downtown department store, I not only didn't sell any of my works, I barely got anyone to even *look* at them. It was at that precise moment that I decided that I was not going to become a famous artist.

After that initial, dismal failure at the Battle of Artist Alley, I packed away my little tubes of Titanium White and Scarlet Lake and poured my can of Turpentine symbolically down the drain. Who was I kidding? I had a better chance at displacing Bud Harrelson at shortstop for the Miracle Mets than becoming a renowned artist.

My furlough from the fine arts arena freed up a large chunk of time that I quickly filled with miscreant behaviors. We started scoping out some of the local taverns and beer joints—from a distance of course— to see what kinds of people patronized them and to view first-hand the effects of alcohol had on them on their way out.

I had gotten an early glimpse a couple of years past escorting my mom to and from her job as bar maid at the E&M Tavern. But any time I got to spend inside the bar was spent playing shuffleboard or pool and plugging the jukebox, so I really never undertook a sociological study of the clientele. I just knew people smelled funny and talked louder the drunker they got. Sometimes they hit each other with pool cues.

We made our rounds of all of Chanute's watering holes—and there were plenty of them at that time. From the Top Hat Club at the north end of town to the Dynamite on the far south side, and everything in between, we observed them all and collectively decided that turning 18 couldn't come soon enough. It looked like, aside from the puking in the parking lots and drunken, bloody fistfights, jolly good fun.

At our age, the closest we could get to being in a real barroom environment was to play pool and/or pinball at the Eight Ball, the local pool hall on East Main. There, we could mingle nearly seamlessly with all of the old timers playing dominoes and the younger men clacking the balls on regulation billiard tables. The place reeked of cigar smoke and chewing tobacco. The bathrooms were worse. Curse words were the language of the day. Much beer was swilled and spilled. In short, it quickly became one of our favorite places to spend money and time.

Additionally, and as if to emphasize the seediness of the joint, we never entered the building from its storefront entrance. We did so, rather, by a rotten-wood sliding door at the very back adjacent to the alley. Was there ever a better way to make an arrival at such a wonderful establishment? I think not.

Many hours and dollars were wasted in that grand emporium of pork rind chips, green felt, cue chalk and spittoons. I wouldn't take any of them back, either.

Another forbidden place that we had long eyed for exploration was the annual Mexican Fiesta. To fully understand the significance of Chanute's version of the celebration of Mexican Independence Day, a brief history lesson is in order. Mexicans first settled in Chanute after the Lawrence, Leavenworth & Galveston Railroad was purchased by the Atchison, Topeka and Santa Fe Railroad in 1880. The ATSF expanded their operations in the city and a fair number of Mexicans were employed by the railroad and relocated to the south end of town.

There they settled in and became an integral part of the community. Beginning in 1918 they celebrated Mexican Independence Day with a festival in their neighborhood, which became known as "Little Mexico." Thereafter, every second weekend in September, so as to get as close as possible to the September 16th Independence Day date, the festival was held to commemorate Mexican heritage with south-of-the-border cuisine, dancing and of course, imbibing.

The program was eventually moved, due to the ever-growing throngs of celebrants, to Santa Fe Park just south of town. Tens of thousands of people came from all over to attend the two-day party. It thus became one of the oldest and largest Mexican Independence Day celebrations in the state of Kansas. It was also one of the few places, we would learn, where one could drink beer right in front of the police and *not* be hassled. They tended to look the other way unless you were causing a problem.

And, as usually happens when there is dancing and drinking, there were occasional problems. Mom had warned me about going out to the Fiesta and cited unverified news stories of beatings, stabbings and general mayhem. None of her scare tactics dissuaded me from making my first visit to the fabled shindig with my cohorts in crime.

Santa Fe Park was a few miles from our neighborhood, so instead of walking or hitching a ride, we hopped a slow-moving southbound freight train out of the ATSF yard and hoped it wouldn't be going too fast to jump off as it passed by Santa Fe Lake to the west of the Fiesta. Luckily, because of yard limit restrictions at the south end of the railroad's complex, the manifest was just picking up speed as we bounded clear just past the trestle over the lake. Catching a faster northbound home later that night would be the real challenge.

For our first Mexican Fiesta and all of the pandemonium predicted by over-reactive parents, it was by all standards, quite a letdown. Based on their stories, I half expected to see crazed Mexicans with handlebar mustachios wearing brightly colored serapes chasing after unsuspecting gringos with large shiny coas. Or maybe a tourist sitting under a bench, his faux sombrero lilting down, hiding his face and reeking of tequila.

Instead, we saw beautiful native Mexican dancers, red and green fresco lights strung from tree to tree, dreamy music emanating from Spanish guitars and blaring horns. The stirring, pungent smell of homemade tacos, burritos, tamales and tostadas being prepared in booths permeated the grounds. People were singing and laughing, clearly enjoying the moment. Attending police and security looked bored. All of the fears of our elders proved wrong—at least this time.

Little did they know that the ride home—yes, by hopping a *much* faster northbound freight train—later that night was infinitely more dangerous.

Fall came early that year, and nowhere in the city was it more evident and on magical display than Highland Street near the Hildebrandt's home. The Scarlet Red Maples and Autumn Purple Ashes that lined the old, wide brick street seemed to be taking on their own personalities while showing off their October finery. Up and down Highland the trees blazed a tableau of deep cadmium orange, eggplant, crimson and umber.

As usual, however, whenever autumn came early in the Midwest, the same trees were nearly always barren and cadaverous by Halloween. We trekked down Highland through clouds of swirling leaves to watch the annual Spook Parade. The grade school procession snaked down Main Street under a threatening sky and a horizon on fire. It seemed like yesterday, yet long ago, when we made the annual pilgrimage downtown dressed as pirates, ghosts and cowboys.

Now too old to even trick or treat, we made our way over to Barker's for chili cones and Cokes. Visible across the street from our table was the Memorial Building, Chanute's all-purpose city facility. The handsome red-brick structure, built in the late 1920's, housed the Police Department, the Fire Department and loads of other city department offices. Municipal Auditorium, also located within the building, was where the annual Christmas Pageants were held.

"Let's go check out the auditorium," I suggested to Jason and Donnie. "I heard that it is haunted."

"No way," Donnie protested. "Besides, it's probably locked up tight."

"Well, I'm gonna go and check it out," I responded, and scooping up the remains of my chili cone, headed out the door. Naturally, the two followed. I knew they couldn't resist a new adventure—even if I did come up with the idea.

Though the three grand entrances were indeed locked, we were able to find a hallway entry door on the third floor west side that was not. We quietly let ourselves in and waited for a moment for our eyes to slowly become acclimated to the dark, cavernous theater. Minus the actors, carolers and parents, the auditorium was dead still and it became possible to hear small, insignificant noises and to pick up weird odors.

We took our seats near the middle of the main level of the theater and sat in total, dread silence. Steam radiators, activated by the cold weather and fed by, I was certain, a monstrous boiler in the basement, clanked and hissed along the walls. The skittering of mice across the floor made our ears perk up. Above the balcony, the lonely wind outside bellowed a mournful song.

The place had a crumbling sensibility to it and smelled musty, mildewed and old. Maybe it was the fabric of the stage curtains or the aisle runners. Perhaps it was the invisible yet piquant vapor emitting from the radiators. Whatever it was, the effect was both and at once morose and cheery.

"This dump ain't haunted," Donnie lamented. "Let's get the hell out of here." As I sat there in the interrupted silence, I imagined Lon Chaney as the Phantom of the Opera swooping down from the overhead chandelier, black cape flapping, bulging eyes ablaze. In my fantasy he grabs Donnie and Jason by their throats and screams, "Do you believe now?" After they have wet their pants he releases them with a warning to never question their friend Michael again. Then cackling maniacally, he disappears behind the stage curtains to await the next stage production.

The walk home took us past thinning groups of trick or treaters racing against the clock and porch lights systematically turning off one by one.

"See ya tomorrow," I said to Jason and Donnie as I veered off across the power plant lawn. Overhead, the moon, slightly past its full stage, emerged from behind dark clouds and slid into full view. I can't be certain, but I think I got a glimpse of The Phantom as he steered his gondola down the canal under my house.

By November, school had de-evolved into a mind-numbing banality of survival. Even the inclusion in Physical Education class of such oddities as Cage Ball and Scooter Wars could not deliver me from my black apathy. Cage Ball made no sense to me—which now explains why I always did so poorly at it. What was gratifying, or even particularly beneficial, about keeping a large ball the size of a zeppelin, in the air? All I wanted to do was pop it. Whenever it rolled my way I usually feigned pushing up against it—letting more talented (and interested) classmates have at it.

Scooter Wars was even worse. The scooters were square and had four wheels at each corner that, like a grocery cart, turned in all directions. The object was to remove your fellow gym classmates from their scooter by whatever means necessary and to become "the last man sitting." This meant kicking, wrestling, pulling, punching (when the teacher wasn't looking) and generally mauling. It might have been more meaningful had we been given knives or side arms.

Actually, it was generally good fun until someone got kicked in the family jewels or lost a tooth. At the very least, someone left with a finger pointing in the wrong direction or a clump of hair missing—later to be found wrapped around one of the wheels. Mopping up a little blood was a common occurrence.

And, like most grocery carts, I seemed to get the scooter with one defective wheel. So not only could my opponents hear me coming—negating that 'surprise' factor—but they could also take advantage of my limited range. To that end, I usually extricated myself from my own scooter—much to the chagrin of my opponents. Like Sugarfoot, they too hated the denial of the kill.

I detested Scooter Wars almost as much as Journalism.

While my supposed writing prowess and numerous school awards for essays, poems and short stories landed me in Journalism at the insistence of and under the stern and matronly auspices of Miss Metheny, I somehow got relegated to "staff artist" shortly after arrival in Room 202.

My artwork for the school paper, hindered by obsolete and archaic tools, was horrendous. Despite my poor attitude, non-existent work ethic and shabby performance, I was soon directed to replicate the winning design for the cover of The Rocket, our school yearbook. It sucked, too, deepening my distrust for nearly all teachers. When I passed on a request to design and create a set for a school play and bailed on a semester-ending Journalism class party, Miss Metheny decried my waste of talent and bemoaned that I was a textbook "underachiever."

Perhaps she was right—at the time. If I'd been allowed to paint in oils the cover for The Rocket, maybe things would have been different. As it was, I submitted zero written contributions to the school paper and only garnered a third place finish in one category—short stories—in the yearbook. Like I had previously with my art supplies, I soon abandoned plans to be the next Robert E. Howard and shelved my typewriter for better days.

On December 1, warrants for the arrest of a few members of a California desert commune known as The Manson Family for the slaughter at the Tate-Polanski and LaBianca homes in suburban Los Angeles were issued. It would be months before the complete, ugly truth evolved. Words scrawled on the walls of the victim's homes in their own blood were purportedly culled from the Beatles "The White Album."

Wow. The good news seemed to virtually seep out of the TV.

On December 6 what was supposed to have been a free rock concert in the vein of Woodstock turned into a violent melee with one stabbing death at Altamont Speedway in northern California. Thus Altamont ironically came to be viewed as the *end* of the hippie era and the *de facto* conclusion of late 60's American youth culture. Peace, love and flowers had been replaced by guns, knives and death. Fear had supplanted courage. It was truly an amazing transformation in such a short time frame.

As Christmas drew near we celebrated Tiny Tim's first birthday and made plans for a festive, if not austere, holiday. It didn't seem quite fair that, just when mom found a job that paid well, she had yet another mouth to feed. I felt guilty about my attitude, but we could never seem to rise above the poverty level. It sucked—and there was nothing I could do about it.

Back at the forced-labor camp known as school, interscholastic basketball had begun, replete with apple-cheeked cheerleaders, packed stands and loud buzzers that screamed victory. In the only time I would ever join any kind of extracurricular club or organization, my friends nominated and elected me captain of one of the intramural basketball teams. I wasn't sure what to make of the dishonor.

Immediately (and ignorantly) I selected my friends and fringe entourage—all of them with no physical abilities other than running from the law—for teammates. The process for picking players based on their athleticism and abilities had not apparently been evident to me. They even let me name our mascot.

In yet another imbecilic move, I christened our team The Ramblers. I chose it based on, in my opinion, our group's habit of 'rambling' around town. Virtually everybody else in school—and especially opposing teams with cooler mascot names like Pythons, Hawks, etc.—imagined the AMC car of the same name. The one that was discontinued in 1969.

And like that Rambler, we were slow, obsolete-looking and destined for the scrap heap of history. We did win a few games, though, as hard as it is for me now to believe. Usually and somewhat predictably, we tended to be on the wrong side of a serious tail-whipping. The Saturday morning walk home was always long and cold after getting severely drubbed. It had always been my contention that intramural sports were the repository for the not-so-physically-talented masses. After the sordid debacle with the Ramblers, I was certain of it.

I therefore added talent scout and manager to my list of failed endeavors—and careers to avoid.

Someone in our group decided that what we needed was some structure, some military-like discipline. Never mind that the war in Viet Nam was still burbling nicely and that in just a few short years we would all be registering for the draft. So we did the next best thing. We joined the Boy Scouts. I should have known what was going to happen. A blind man could've seen it coming.

With no previous experience, say as a Cub Scout for instance, to prep us for the higher calling of Boy Scouts, it was painfully obvious to everyone else that we were fish out of water. Our stay in Troop 100 was such a short time that we never even got to order our official Khaki Boy Scout shirts, let alone wear them.

The list of grievances was long and painful. We screwed up the pledge, made fun of the 'dorks' in our troop, cursed like drunken sailors and Donnie smoked like a chimney outside before and after every wasted meeting. In short, we were everything most scouts weren't—lazy, contemptuous and negative—all with a "can't do" attitude for icing. We struggled learning how to tie their knots and felt no inclination to walk old ladies across the street—except for Mrs. Pendarvis. They didn't give out Merit badges for bringing *Playboy* to overnight camping trips, either.

We were in and out of Troop 100 at the Otterbein Methodist Church faster than you could say "Eagle Scout."

Exactly one week before Christmas we bought our holiday tree from Farmer's Discount Center, the sprawling get-everything-here store on West Cherry. You could buy nearly anything you wanted in that store. From wigs to wrist watches to groceries to salt blocks, barbed wire and cattle feed, if you required it, they generally had it. Even Christmas trees. We found ours in the "wall of shame," that curious annual mid-December line-up of forlorn trees leaning up against the storefront, all looking for a home for the holidays.

I guess I should have been grateful that we were buying a tree in the first place. It was a far cry from the not-too-distant old days where we either went out and cut down a Cedar or stole one from outside of one of the stores or tree lots. We nicknamed the latter "moonlight trees," reflecting the time of day that we pilfered them. Still, brushing snow from the sparse and spindly branches of our Douglas Fir revealed that it bore more than a passing resemblance to the Charlie Brown tree on TV.

I spent most of Christmas vacation lying around and watching all of the holiday specials on TV—*Frosty the Snowman*, *How the Grinch Stole Christmas*, etc. It sure beat fighting with Miss Metheny, getting roughed up in Phys Ed and worrying about a myriad of things I had absolutely no control over.

Our plans for crashing any number of New Year's parties also eventually evaporated when Donnie went down with the flu. Sickness had a way of racing through the Hildebrandt home like an ammonia leak in a meat packing plant. Jason then decided to go to Kansas City and visit family, so I was left with little sis and a cheerless, drying tree bereft of presents.

On that special night when most people were out having fun and ringing in the New Year with the one (or ones) they love, I sat alone, unless you count a fossilized Guy Lombardo babbling on the TV, in the darkened living room. It was, in retrospect, fitting that I surrounded myself with solitude on one of the noisiest nights of the year. The utter silence was a perfect backdrop for long-overdue self-examination.

The sixties were gone and a new decade lay ahead—with all of its uncertainties. There was nothing I could do to change anything in the past, but I was confident in the knowledge that there was plenty I could do to alter events yet to happen. I was angry at my father for abandoning my sisters and me, but I was grateful for the love of my remaining family. I was worried about my grades, all the while knowing I had in me the power to alter their course.

It's funny, for as much as I couldn't wait for the sixties to end, with all of the national discord and personal anxieties, I wasn't exactly eager to see what the new decade might bring. This dichotomy of emotions made my head swim. The monotonous blinking Christmas tree lights didn't help, either.

Entering a new decade is quite different than entering a new year. In 1969, for me, it had all of the sensation of free-falling from a burning high rise to rescuers with a large inflated air mattress on the street below. In order to jump, I had to trust that I could hit the mattress.

I looked up at the starburst wall clock in the kitchen. It read 12:05 AM. Mom was at work making bombs, Tim was at the sitter's and little sis was asleep, curled up in a fetal position on the floor in front of the TV.

I opened the back porch door and could hear fireworks going off in the distance. People were celebrating. Across the street, a switcher pushed a boxcar into a long row of stationary freight cars with a resounding crash. Sleet began pinging off the roof.

I was alive, awake and as usual—searching for answers that rarely came easy.

It was 1970.

Afterword

We were, as countless generations claimed both before and after us in the 1960s, "different." Kids were different. Parents were different. In some ways, after the staid and starched 1950s, the decade that followed could arguably be considered the anecdotal end of innocence. Certainly, undeniably, it was a time like no other.

I have always opined that life, somewhat like a train station, is comprised of many arrivals and departures—and for every tank town we pause at on our journey, there are countless others we pass by as whistle stops. A part of me is still cemented, for good or bad, in that decade of war, assassination, political upheaval, flower children and paisley pants.

Visiting Chanute, my hometown, these days is much like catching up with a kindly old uncle whom I haven't seen for years. At once he seems familiar yet oddly different. And it appears that we have virtually nothing in common anymore—though that's probably not a bad thing. Though he is aging and his health is waning a bit, uncle is in a rigid state of denial and insists that "everything is okay." Like him, I want to believe everything's okay, too.

In 2009, the population of Chanute dipped to 8,854.00. That's nearly 2,000 less than when we lived there in 1960 at its peak. That statistic in and of itself is neither good nor bad until you consider that there are fewer people paying higher taxes for schools and infrastructure improvements.

There may be more people dead in the ground at the local cemeteries now than those living in the city itself.

Of all of the changes decades have wrought, one of the first things I notice when I go back to the city these days is the *silence*. Main Street was long ago reduced down from two-lane to one-lane with slanted parking, reducing the congestion—and also the hustle and bustle—of automobile traffic. Shuttered storefronts rival active businesses for space and appear as rotten teeth in a once-pretty smile. U.S. 169, which in its day cut a path directly through town with its voluminous truck caravans, was re-routed in 1984 about five miles west of town. The roar of Peterbuilts and Macks hauling goods and commerce were thus quieted.

With the disappearance of the truck route through the heart of the city, whole retail enterprises went into the proverbial ditch, including motels, restaurants, grocery stores, and gas stations.

Mid-America Refinery's shift whistle was silenced in the early 1981 when the company declared bankruptcy and closed its doors forever. The site later became an EPA Superfund cleanup project—our own slightly different version, I guess, of Love Canal.

The Santa Fe Railroad, for a time the largest employer in Chanute, pulled up stakes in 1990. The branch line from Iola, 17 miles north, to Tulsa, Oklahoma, 150 miles south was purchased by Watco and a new chapter of short line service was thereby established. Unneeded by its new owner, and with the absence of through trains and switchers, the large hump yard now sits in tomb-like silence amidst ribbons of rusted rails and overgrown weeds. In what seemed to me to be a comically symbolic move, they even turned off the yard lights that illuminated the complex.

One could throw a stuffed dummy from the yard light today and I can almost assure you that no one would notice.

With through rail traffic basically cut off, the large grain elevators at Chanute Grain & Seed were soon dismantled, then rebuilt and moved to 21st Street to give the new short line operator better access. Long a harbinger of summer, the *whoosh* of the wheat granules being transferred to the rail cars is now no more—unless you are a duck traversing the wetlands area near 21st Street.

Perhaps the most distressing of all of the silences, though, is the absence of the laughter of children swimming at the old city pool. Norma Maring retired following her 50th year as pool manager in 2006 and after her departure the facility closed due to "repair" issues. A new "aquatic center" has been built on the property where the city High School once sat—before it was demolished in 2008. Fittingly, the new pool was named in honor of the Marings.

Children still splash and squeal with delight—but words cannot properly describe how different it is without the Marings there lording over the old oval.

Recent visits turned up no kids playing pickup football or baseball games in any of the various places we used to haunt. Indeed, one of our favorite fields was just to the north of Hans' Flowers. That business expanded a number of years ago and where I once broke tackles for long touchdown runs on chilly Saturday mornings in the fall they now maintain and transplant flowers in a greenhouse.

A new high school was constructed several years ago south of town. More recently the local school district voted to centralize the elementary schools and combine all of the Chanute grade school children into one new structure. It was constructed near the site of the new high school.

In retrospect, it was probably a good idea that might save the district untold dollars in the future. All of the 'neighborhood' elementary schools, the newest of which were 50 years old, were beginning to show serious signs of bedrock failure. It was clear that a massive amount of money was going to be required not just to update and upgrade the facilities, but just to keep them from decaying any further.

As it is now possible for all children in Chanute to literally be with each other from Kindergarten to graduation, lost forever is the mystery and anticipatory thrill of the other 'kids' converging at Royster Junior High for 7th grade. The era of the neighborhood schools, sadly not unlike that of the neighborhood grocery stores, has now passed into the historical mists of my hometown. The joy of *walking* to school through a surprise spring thundershower or sliding expertly on snow-packed sidewalks will not be memories for the current crop of students.

Royster Junior High School, freshly constructed when I first got there as a fresh-faced 7th grader in the Fall of 1967, is still there and has been added onto a number of times. It is now a middle school.

All of the fine eateries noted within this book are, not surprisingly, gone. It is to this day a very predatory and small-margin business where swift change is the norm. There are, of course, a number of very nice restaurants in current-day Chanute, but none have the curb service charm of the old A & W Root beer stand on south Santa Fe nor the addictive fried aroma of The Chicken Shack, where even the Colonel would have probably clamored for the recipe.

Chains such as the Sonic Drive-In, Hardees and McDonald's soon moved in and many of the local mom and pop greasy spoons simply vanished from the scene, including Barker's Dairy Bar—taking with it the esteemed chili cone.

Of all five houses we lived in during the 1960s, three have survived. The very first and second homes we roosted in are gone. The West Main house where I battled everyday with Sugarfoot, the maniacal goat, was leveled in the early 1980s to make way for the re-routing of U.S. 169. I often wonder if old 'Foot's ghost haunts the area. I can imagine her standing on the bluffs, looking down on the four-lane highway, itching to ram any of the offending vehicles.

The two-story clapboard house on South Evergreen with the beautiful Catalpa tree standing guard in the yard was torn down in the 1980s. A vacant lot exists where we once had our collective photograph taken prior to Easter service on a windswept March day. Warner's Market, the corner grocery store just a few hundred feet to the south that became our de facto gathering place, is still standing, though it has been idle for many years.

Many of the buildings that housed the old mom and pop grocery stores are surprisingly still there—some empty, some having taken on a new lives. My favorite of the bunch, Jeff's Foodliner, is long gone, however, and is now a gravel parking lot on the northwest corner of Main and Grant Streets.

As usually happens with most childhood friendships, differing interests and directions often divide and finally separate people from their moorings. We drift apart—sometimes never to see each other again and other times to re-unite at some point down the proverbial road. I did not retain many of the relationships with boyhood friends described in this book. Still, decades have not ebbed the solidarity I felt with them during those turbulent years.

I can still see their faces and hear their voices—frozen in time. In fact, whenever I venture to reunions, I have a tendency to see all of my friends and classmates as the kids they once were. It is a strange and somewhat perverse gift to be able to look past the wrinkles, gray hair and added (and in some cases, subtracted) weight to be able to see the cute girl with the shiny pony tail, the skinny boy with the crew cut—as if they'd never aged. I call it "The Dorian Gray Factor."

The roll call for things that *have* changed, though, continues.

The grand old bridge that spanned the Neosho River at Austin was eventually closed to automobile traffic, and then closed, period. A section of the bridge was eventually moved to Santa Fe Park, and the rest was scrapped. If I take the time and allow myself to drift, I can still hear the thump-thump of cars driving across the timbers over the span. In my reverie I am still sitting on the bridge listening to the riffles below on a humid June night, the air ablaze with fireflies.

The cable that we once crossed the river hand-over-hand near Brown Wells Dam is gone. So too is the old MKT railroad trestle spanning Village Creek where we once were champion bullhead fishermen. The old slaughterhouse where we took shots at each other with BB guns was torn down many years ago. Even the places where the railroad tracks themselves once were have yielded to Mother Nature. She is clearly taking back what was once hers.

Johnson Hospital, already old and abandoned when we conducted our "run with the transients," has been gone for decades. Greenwood Cemetery is still there, but closed to the public for most of the time. The tall ATSF yard light tower from which we threw Drooper, the stuffed dummy, to an untimely death still exists but access to the top was curtailed when a portion of the ladder was removed near ground level.

The drainage canal, where we often found ourselves immediately following thunderstorms, is still there, but during recent visits to the city I never once saw any kids tramping through it. Looking at it even now, 45 years later, temps me to jump down and start trekking across it's expanse of broken glass and washed-out refuse.

The Tioga Hotel, decaying and on shaky legs during the 1960s, would undergo some very remarkable changes over the next 50 years. It closed for a time, housed ATSF railroad workers, reopened as "Continental Inn" in 1978, was used for offices and shops in the 1980s, and was for a short time an assisted living facility in 1990. In 2006 new owners refurbished the grand old lady, including exposing some of the original plaster and pegboard as well as restoring the original tin ceilings. A restaurant was added and new life was breathed into her 33 hotel rooms and 21 apartments.

Though I have been a paying customer on recent visits to the city, I still have not gotten to the roof of the hotel to look down with the grotesques. Not yet, anyway...

Joyland Park, one of our favorite summer getaways in Wichita, was recently closed and the prospects for re-opening it look very bleak. A victim of socioeconomic neighborhood transition, vandalism has run rampant in the park and thieves have stolen everything that wasn't nailed down—and in some cases, even what *was* nailed down, including the "Sit Down" sign that marked the summit of the Rollercoaster.

Peoples Theater hung on and eventually was sold and re-named Chanute Cinema. Recently the old building, where we once pelted unsuspecting patrons from the balcony with all types of sticky candy, was razed to the ground for a parking lot. A new theater was built across the street, and while it is impressive and contains as much state-of-the-art equipment as the owners could afford, it has absolutely none of the decaying ambiance that Peoples infected us young movie-goers with many moons ago.

The Neo-Cha met a fate similar to most drive-in movie theaters across the land. It closed in the late 1970s and there is now a green field where once cars teeming with people watched a flickering, giant screen and listened to dated double-features through tinny speakers on stands.

One by one, all of my family members packed up and moved away. I was the last to leave in 1990. Mom, child of the Great Depression, applier of Mercurochrome, baker of mayonnaise cakes and assembler of bombs, moved away 25 years ago and is now retired. The rest of the family followed one by one.

After 41 years, I finally got to see my father again in 2005 when I stopped at his home on a business trip through south Texas. We spent the day looking at old photos and reminiscing—there was no time for opening old wounds or pointing fingers of blame. Indeed, three short years later I would attend his funeral.

Amidst all of the expected change spanning five decades, some things have remained charmingly undisturbed in Chanute. For instance, the reassuring peal of the Presbyterian Church bell still rings out every hour on the hour. While that might seem small and inconsequential, I can assure you that to the old visitor who once lived there, it is a very welcoming sound that conjures up youthful fancies.

Nature's landmarks, the Neosho River and Santa Fe Lake still beckon fishermen young and old alike. Canadian Geese still honk loudly as they ascend the thermals high above Chanute every autumn. Suicide Hill remains, though it looks far less foreboding now than it did those frosty fall and winter mornings of years gone by. For everything that changes, I guess there are probably just as many that take on a comforting timelessness.

The book you are now finishing represents just a snapshot—a mere microcosm in the expansive history of myself, family, friends and my hometown. It connects several points on a life compass, an intersection of time, circumstance and people.

Had I been a Chanute resident in 1885, I might have written about how it was prudent in those days when venturing downtown to always remember to strap on one's sidearm. I could have described the horses tied to their hitching posts up and down Central Street. Later I would have celebrated the arrival of the first motor car in town while bemoaning the disappearance of blacksmiths shops and livery and boarding barns.

I might have pontificated on the 100-year oil boom that turned into a 10-year bust and permanently changed the direction Chanute would take.

Instead of scribing about packs of children chasing after the city mosquito fogger, I might have detailed how they ran behind the water wagon wetting down the dirt and new brick streets being laid in the city. If I had been writing about my hometown in the 1930's I could have explored the rumor that Bonnie and Clyde spent the night in the Manhattan Hotel on Main Street near the railroad tracks. Purportedly, they came in at night under aliases and paid the deskman and bellhop "plenty" to keep silent.

They were gone before the morning light.

Had I been just a tad younger I could have written about the devastating effects of the '51 flood and how post-war boom in America was reflected in Chanute with new businesses opening up and homes being built at record paces.

That I came to write about the 1960s in my hometown first began as a gift to my kids—a way, if you will, to give them more history about their father as a youth as well as describe what it felt like to be there at that place at that specific time. In writing this book I learned much about myself, too.

I had originally thought that the memoir would be a fun, sticky-sweet stroll down memory lane. I hadn't prepared for the impact that some of the world events seemingly had on our lives in that little Midwestern town. Living in a literal cocoon during one of the most distressing times in American history had a unique effect on us all—young and old alike.

I watched my mother search, sometimes clumsily, for acceptance and love while at the same time trying to raise a family of three—then four—all against a backdrop of a society seemingly coming apart at the seams. I saw young people die in my hometown—car accidents, a lightning strike, drownings.

Local boys perished in Viet Nam. We heard about it from neighbors and friends and then watched as their names were engraved on the wall in front of the Memorial Building alongside all of the other city sons who never returned from the previous wars.

It was all very paradoxical. The best way I can describe it would be like listening to a violent maelstrom from inside a thin-walled hut. You know it's very bad out there, but you also feel somewhat safe inside with your family and friends.

To this day, I still get the chills whenever I hear the eerie, haunting intro to the Four Tops masterpiece "Reach Out, I'll be There" on the radio, still crane my neck to see a fully restored GTO race past me on the interstate and smile to myself at the relics of my youth on sale at flea markets and antique shops all across America.

With the unrepentant passage of time, all of those things take on a richer, deeper meaning.

For sure, though, and as the old saying goes, you can't go back home—at least not the way it once was. You don't get your seat back. Nor should you want it back. I am a strident believer that looking back is okay—even healthy—as long as you continue to look ahead with equal, if not greater fervor.

If I could just find a place that still made chili cones...

ABOUT THE AUTHOR

Michael Winslow grew up in Chanute, Kansas, and has contributed essays and articles to the *Chanute Tribune* and *RailNews*. He currently lives with his wife in rural Parker County, Texas.

LaVergne, TN USA
04 January 2011
211120LV00001B/230/P